café
food
at home

café
food
at home

GAEL OBERHOLZER

photography by
craig fraser and warren heath

dedicated to Cathrin

Struik Publishers
(a division of New Holland Publishing
(South Africa) (Pty) Ltd)
Cornelis Struik House
80 McKenzie Street
Cape Town 8001
South Africa
New Holland Publishing is a member
of the Johnnic Publishing Group

First published in 2002
10 9 8 7 6 5 4 3 2 1

Publishing manager: Linda de Villiers
Editor: Joy Clack
Designer: Petal Palmer
Design assistant: Sean Robertson
Colour consultant: Farouk Abrahams
Photographers: Craig Fraser and
    Warren Heath
Food stylist: Justine Kiggan
Reproduction by Hirt & Carter Cape
    (Pty) Ltd
Printed and bound by
    Tien Wah Press (Pte) Ltd, Singapore

ISBN 1 86872 717 3

www.struik.co.za
Log on to our photographic website
www.imagesofafrica.co.za
for an African experience.

Thank you to the following for
supplying props:
Bright House, LIM, Yellow Door and
Hope: Traditional Garden Furniture.

Author's acknowledgements

With thanks to all the staff and
customers (who have become friends)
at Gourmet Coffee House; to Paul at
the Village Bistro for inspiring me to
get back into the kitchen; to Sonya
for her help; to Justin and Robin for
the chilli ideas; to all the people
who've helped put this book together;
and to my family.

contents

introduction **7**

essentials **8**

soups **38**

salads **52**

wraps **70**

specials **90**

sweet things **116**

index **127**

introduction

No recipe is a new recipe. Whether it comes from a traditional dish handed down through generations or from a gourmet chef's recipe book, every dish is a variation of a variation.

As a chef, I take ideas from cookbooks, exploit culinary tips from friends or glean tastes from a corner café on the streets of Israel. But I also believe in putting my own touch into everything I cook to make it unique and my own. And this is what *Café Food at Home* is all about.

Café Food at Home is a practical book that starts you off with some basic, essential recipes and then gives you a few ideas on how to make these work for you. This is not so that you can diligently reproduce each recipe step by step; instead it provides you with a launching pad to try your own ideas. Cooking is about experimenting. It's about substituting, swapping, lending, borrowing, using your imagination and taking risks. Start with familiar staples like bangers and mash, but this time, mash your potatoes with cream, a hint of rosemary and some grated pecorino cheese. Add a couple of tablespoons of red wine to your gravy, choose a quality sausage and you'll lift that humble pub fare from the bar counter to a gourmet café's table.

So take these recipes, add what you know, remember what your mother taught you, and roll up your sleeves and create your own unique variations of my variations.

Gael

"Even if you know
only one recipe,
you can make it work
for lots of other dishes."

essentials

basic tomato SAUCE

serves 6

2 onions, finely chopped

2 large cloves garlic, crushed and
  chopped

2 Tbsp (30 ml) olive oil

3 x 400 g cans whole, peeled tomatoes

a few sprigs fresh oregano, chopped

4 tsp (20 ml) Basil Pesto (page 26)
  or a handful of fresh basil leaves

a large pinch of chopped fresh parsley

salt and freshly ground black
  pepper to taste

1–2 Tbsp (15–30 ml) brown sugar

(photograph on page 9)

Gently sauté the onions and garlic in the olive oil, then add the remaining ingredients. Bring to the boil, reduce heat and simmer gently for 1–2 hours. Taste and adjust the seasoning. If the sauce is too acidic, add more sugar (the sauce, however, should not be sweet).

"This sauce forms the basis of many dishes in this book. By adding a little pesto, Chilli Sauce (page 11) or even Fiery Moroccan Paste (page 19), you can transform it to suit an even greater variety of dishes. This sauce is ideal for pastas, phyllo fillings, soups, stews or gravies, to mention just a few. If made in large quantities, the sauce can be frozen for up to three months."

chilli

makes 3 cups (750 ml)

**125 g assorted fresh chillies, stalks
removed and roughly chopped**
65 g coarse dried red chillies
125 g brown sugar
1 thick slice of fresh lemon
**2 cups (500 ml) brown or
white vinegar**
10 g dried mixed herbs
1 tsp (5 ml) salt
65 g chopped garlic
¾ cup (180 ml) olive oil
½ cup (125 ml) ginger beer
½ cup (125 ml) sherry
**a small pinch of chopped fresh
coriander or mint (optional)**

Place the chillies, sugar, slice of lemon and vinegar in a heavy-based saucepan. Bring to the boil and simmer gently for 20 minutes. Strain the liquid, reserving 1 Tbsp (15 ml) of the chilli stock. Discard the slice of lemon. Blend the chilli pulp in the blender with the reserved stock. Return the blended pulp to the saucepan and add the remaining ingredients. Bring to the boil, then remove from heat, add the coriander or mint (if using) and leave to cool for a few minutes. Bottle the chilli sauce while it is still hot so that it creates a vacuum and will last longer.

"A versatile sauce that can be added to any dish to spice things up a bit."

essentials 11

mushroom
SAUCE

makes about 4 cups (1 litre)

2 tsp (10 ml) olive oil
80 g butter
1 small onion, finely chopped
1 clove garlic, crushed and chopped
250 g button mushrooms, sliced
a pinch of dried mixed herbs
a pinch of chopped fresh parsley
6 Tbsp (90 ml) white wine
½ cup (125 ml) cake flour
1½ cups (375 ml) milk
1 tsp (5 ml) Marmite
a few drops of soy sauce
salt and freshly ground black
   pepper to taste
6 Tbsp (90 ml) fresh cream

Heat the oil and butter in a saucepan and sauté the onion, garlic, mushrooms, mixed herbs and parsley. Deglaze with the white wine and reduce. When the wine has almost evaporated, remove from heat and stir in the flour (the consistency should be rather pasty). Return to low heat and add a little milk at a time until you have a smooth paste. Add the rest of the milk and bring to the boil, stirring continuously. Add the Marmite, soy sauce and a pinch of pepper. Taste and adjust the salt. Add the cream, bring to the boil and remove from heat. This sauce can be frozen.

"Serve with Burgers (page 94) or Phyllo Wraps (pages 99 and 101)."

béchamel (WHITE) SAUCE

makes about 4 cups (1 litre)

80 g butter

80 g cake flour

about 4 cups (1 litre) milk

¼ tsp (1 ml) prepared English mustard

a pinch of grated nutmeg

salt and freshly ground black
   pepper to taste

a pinch of chopped fresh parsley

Melt the butter in a heavy-based pan over low heat. Stir in the flour with a wooden spoon or whisk until the butter absorbs all the flour. Add a little milk at a time until you have a smooth paste. Add the rest of the milk, whisking all the time. Increase the heat and bring to the boil, stirring continuously. Stir in the remaining ingredients.

thai paste

green thai paste
makes about 6–8 Tbsp (90–120 ml)

1 tsp (5 ml) cumin seeds

1 Tbsp (15 ml) coriander seeds

10–12 large fresh green chillies, seeded and very finely chopped

1 Tbsp (15 ml) fresh ginger, very finely chopped

4 spring onions, very finely shredded

4 cloves garlic, crushed and chopped

2 blades lemon grass, minced

vegetable oil

a large handful of fresh coriander, chopped

1 tsp (5 ml) shrimp paste

½ tsp (2.5 ml) turmeric

2 tsp (10 ml) salt

½ tsp (2.5 ml) white pepper

Roast the cumin and coriander seeds for a few minutes in a pan. Allow to cool, then crush the seeds to a fine powder with a rolling pin and set aside. Over low heat, sauté the chillies, ginger, spring onions, garlic and lemon grass in a little oil with the coriander and shrimp paste for a few minutes. Remove from heat and add the turmeric, salt and pepper. Place the mixture in a blender with a little more oil and process until a smooth paste is formed. The paste can be refrigerated for up to a week, or can be frozen for a couple of months.

red thai paste
makes about 6–8 Tbsp (90–120 ml)

Use the same ingredients and method as for the Green Thai Paste, but replace the green chillies with red chillies and add 4 tsp (20 ml) dried crushed red chillies that have been soaked in boiling water for 30 minutes.

HOME-MADE
thai sauce

makes about 3 cups (750 ml)

When making red Thai sauce, go easy on the paste as the red chillies are hotter than the green ones. Remember — you can always add more to taste, but once you've added you can never take out. This sauce can be frozen for many months.

4–5 Tbsp (60–75 ml) Green or Red Thai Paste (page 15)
2 x 400 ml cans coconut milk
1 sweet potato (about 200 g), peeled and thinly sliced
a squeeze of lemon juice and a bit of rind
2 lime leaves
a handful of fresh basil or 1 Tbsp (15 ml) Basil Pesto (page 26)
2–3 drops of fish sauce
a large handful of fresh coriander
salt to taste
2–3 drops of soy sauce

Place all the ingredients in a saucepan over medium-high heat, stirring until the paste has dissolved. Do not let it boil. Reduce heat and simmer gently to allow the sauce to reduce and the sweet potato to cook. If the sauce is too hot for your taste, add a little more coconut milk, but if you prefer it more fiery, add a little more paste.

café food
AT HOME

home-made Thai sauce

teriyaki
SAUCE

makes 3 cups (750 ml)

1 cup (250 ml) water
1 cup (250 ml) soy sauce
1 cup (250 ml) red wine
a dash of sherry
2 cloves garlic, crushed and chopped
5-cm piece fresh ginger, peeled and
   chopped

Mix all the ingredients together and use a funnel to decant it into a bottle. Seal. Always give it a good shake before using.

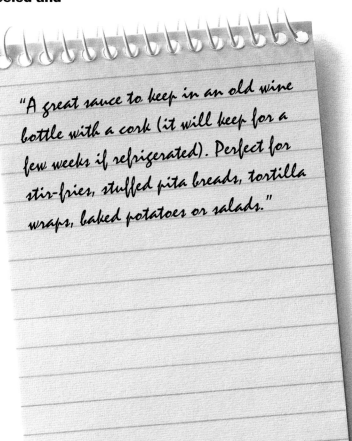

"A great sauce to keep in an old wine bottle with a cork (it will keep for a few weeks if refrigerated). Perfect for stir-fries, stuffed pita breads, tortilla wraps, baked potatoes or salads."

FIERY
moroccan paste

makes 4 cups (1 litre)

A fiery condiment ideal for almost anything. I love to spoon this into soups, pastas, over chicken, lamb and seafood or serve it on the side with eggs.

200 g dried coarse red chillies, soaked in boiling water
50 g whole dried red chillies (with stalks), soaked in boiling water (optional)
6–8 cloves garlic, crushed and finely chopped
¼ cup (60 ml) salt
1 cup (250 ml) ground coriander
⅔ cup (160 ml) ground cumin
1½ cups (375 ml) olive oil
a large handful of chopped fresh coriander
a pinch of turmeric

Combine all the ingredients together in a mixing bowl and mix to a smooth paste. This paste will keep in the refrigerator for up to a month and can also be frozen.

tzatziki
(CUCUMBER SALSA)

serves 4

A great condiment for curries, mezze platters, sandwiches, stir-fries and tortilla wraps.

1 English cucumber (about 15 cm long)
1 clove garlic, crushed and finely
   chopped
a small handful of fresh coriander,
   chopped
1 cup (250 ml) plain yoghurt
salt and freshly ground black
   pepper to taste

Cut the cucumber in half lengthways, remove the seeds, and cut in half again. Thinly slice the cucumber and toss it with the remaining ingredients. Serve chilled.

café food
20
AT HOME

tzatziki

tomato

serves 4

2 large, ripe red tomatoes, finely chopped
1 small onion, finely chopped
1 clove garlic, crushed and chopped
1–2 Tbsp (15–30 ml) Chilli Sauce (page 11)
a handful of fresh coriander, chopped
salt and freshly ground black
   pepper to taste

Mix all the ingredients together in a bowl
and adjust seasoning to taste. Serve chilled.

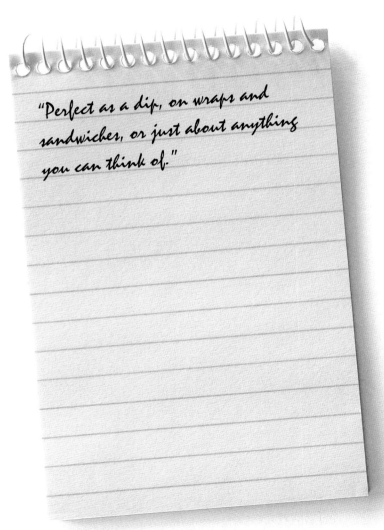

"Perfect as a dip, on wraps and sandwiches, or just about anything you can think of."

hummus

I enjoy this dip in a fillet wrap, on a sandwich, as a dip with roast lamb or even with a stir-fry.

300 g chickpeas, soaked overnight
¼ tsp (1 ml) Fiery Moroccan Paste
  (page 19)
1½ Tbsp (22.5 ml) tahini
1 tsp (5 ml) crushed garlic
¼ cup (60 ml) olive oil
a squeeze of lemon juice to taste
salt and freshly ground black pepper

Drain the chickpeas, cover with fresh water and boil for about 10 minutes. Reduce heat and simmer for about 1 hour, or until soft. Drain, reserving a little of the liquid. Place the chickpeas in a blender with the Moroccan paste, tahini and garlic and process to a smooth purée, adding the oil and lemon juice gradually. Taste and adjust the seasoning. If you prefer it a bit thinner, add some of the reserved liquid. Serve chilled.

guacamole

serves 6

3 ripe avocados, peeled and pip removed
1 small onion, finely chopped
1 ripe tomato, finely chopped
1 Tbsp (15 ml) freshly squeezed
   lemon juice
a large pinch of chopped fresh coriander
1 large Jalapeño chilli, finely chopped
salt and freshly ground black
   pepper to taste
½ tsp (2.5 ml) crushed garlic

Mash the avocados, then add the remaining ingredients and season to taste. Avocado discolours when exposed to air so bury the pip in the dip and cover. Remove the pip just before serving.

pestos

basil PESTO

makes about 1 cup (250 ml)

100 g fresh basil leaves, washed
½ cup (125 ml) olive oil
4 Tbsp (30 g) pine kernels or toasted flaked almonds
2 cloves garlic, crushed and finely chopped
60 g parmesan or pecorino cheese, grated
a little freshly squeezed lemon juice
salt and freshly ground black pepper

Whizz the basil leaves, olive oil, pine kernels or almonds and garlic in a blender until you have a smooth paste. Gradually add the cheese, a few drops of lemon juice and seasoning to taste.

"Basil, olive and sun-dried tomato pesto can be used to liven up a variety of dishes. Spoon into pasta or salads, in phyllo fillings, over roasted vegetables, in mayonnaise and sauces, or in any dish with which you want to experiment. Pesto should have a moist but firm consistency. These pestos keep very well in a sealed container or they can be frozen."

sun-dried tomato
PESTO

makes about 1 cup (250 ml)

100 g sun-dried tomatoes
1½ cups (375 ml) boiling water
castor sugar to taste
salt and freshly ground black
** pepper to taste**
2 cloves garlic, crushed and chopped
6 Tbsp (90 ml) olive oil
a large pinch of chopped fresh parsley

Soak the tomatoes in the boiling water with a little sugar, a pinch of salt and pepper for 1 hour or longer. Drain, but reserve some of the liquid stock. Process the tomatoes, garlic and a little of the oil until a smooth paste is formed, adding a little stock. Mix in the parsley and taste to adjust the seasoning. You may have to add a little more sugar, but be careful not to make it sweet.

   If you want to keep the sun-dried tomatoes whole, just throw all the ingredients, except the olive oil, in a bowl and soak for 1 hour or more. Drain, then add the olive oil. Taste and season if necessary.

black olive
PESTO

makes about 1 cup (250 ml)

1 cup (250 ml) pitted black olives
10 capers
1 clove garlic, crushed and chopped
1 Tbsp (15 ml) freshly squeezed lemon
** juice and a little zest**
¼ cup (60 ml) olive oil
freshly ground black pepper

Chop the olives, capers and garlic. Grate the lemon zest finely and add it to the olives, capers and garlic. Add the oil, freshly ground black pepper and a generous squeeze of lemon juice.

essentials 27

BEST-EVER
vinaigrette

makes 5 cups (1.25 litres)

1 tsp (5 ml) prepared English mustard
2 cloves garlic, crushed and chopped
1 cup (250 ml) mayonnaise
4 tsp (20 ml) finely chopped fresh herbs
½ tsp (2.5 ml) salt
1 tsp (5 ml) freshly ground black pepper
1 cup (250 ml) red-wine vinegar
3 Tbsp (45 ml) honey
5 tsp (25 ml) soy sauce
1 cup (250 ml) water
5 tsp (25 ml) red wine
1 cup (250 ml) olive oil
1 cup (250 ml) cold-pressed sunflower oil

Mix all the ingredients together, except the oils. Whisk in the oils by hand, a little at a time. Mix until the oil blends well with the rest of the ingredients. This dressing lasts for 2–3 weeks if kept in the refrigerator.

vinaigrette WITH SUN-DRIED TOMATO

makes 1 cup (250 ml)

Try this variation of Best-ever Vinaigrette, it's superb.

1 cup (250 ml) Best-ever Vinaigrette
6–8 sun-dried tomatoes

Slice the sun-dried tomatoes into thin strips and add to the vinaigrette. Leave to stand for about 15 minutes before using.

CATHRIN'S
yoghurt dressing

makes 1 cup (250 ml)

1 cup (250 ml) plain yoghurt
a pinch of chopped fresh parsley
2 cloves garlic, crushed and chopped
a generous squeeze of lemon juice
2 Tbsp (30 ml) honey
salt and freshly ground black pepper

Mix all the ingredients together and adjust the seasoning to taste.

CATHRIN'S
lemon dressing

makes about 1½ cups (375 ml)

1 cup (250 ml) fresh lemon juice
3–4 Tbsp (45–60 ml) honey
2 Tbsp (30 ml) water
½ tsp (2.5 ml) salt
½ tsp (2.5 ml) ground black pepper
a pinch of dried mixed herbs
a dash of prepared mustard
⅓ cup (80 ml) olive oil
½ tsp (2.5 ml) crushed garlic

Mix all the ingredients together, except the oil. Whisk in the oil slowly until well blended. This dressing can be kept in the refrigerator for up to two weeks. Allow the dressing to come to room temperature before serving.

roasted vegetables
WITH RED-WINE VINEGAR

serves 6–8 (makes 8 cups)

Roasted vegetables can be used in salads and pastas, on sandwiches or simply as a side dish or snack. The vegetables can be kept in the refrigerator for up to five days.

1 onion, roughly chopped

2 red peppers, seeded and thickly sliced

2 yellow peppers, seeded and thickly sliced

250 g baby marrows, sliced diagonally or lengthways

125 g baby gem squash, halved

2–4 cloves garlic, peeled

250 g baby corn spears

125 g cherry tomatoes

125 g button mushrooms

olive oil to drizzle

salt and freshly ground black pepper to sprinkle

1 Tbsp (15 ml) dried mixed herbs

red-wine vinegar to drizzle

Preheat the oven to 180 °C (350 °F). Place all the vegetables in a roasting pan, drizzle with olive oil and sprinkle with seasoning and herbs. Roast for 20–25 minutes. Drizzle with the red-wine vinegar while still hot. Serve hot or cold.

"You can use other vegetables such as butternut, sweet potato or baby carrots. If you want to use brinjals, be sure to blanch them before adding them to the raw vegetables."

roasted butternut

serves 4–6 (makes 6 cups)

When roasted with chilli, this versatile starch can transform many dishes. It can be served on a salad with plain yoghurt, in phyllo pastry, soups and pasta or with roasted vegetables.

2 large butternuts, peeled and cubed
4–6 Tbsp (60–90 ml) olive oil to drizzle
2–4 Tbsp (30–60 ml) Fiery Moroccan
  Paste (page 19) or Chilli Sauce (page 11)
a large pinch of dried oregano
salt and freshly ground black
  pepper to sprinkle

Preheat the oven to 180 °C (350 °F).
Mix all the ingredients together in a
roasting tray and roast for 30–40 minutes.

café food
AT HOME

FLOUR.
tortilla

makes 6–8

You can buy tortillas from most supermarkets, but if you have the time and energy, try making them yourself.

1½ cups (375 ml) sifted cake flour
1 cup (250 ml) sifted maize meal
a pinch of salt
1 cup (250 ml) warm water

Combine the flour, maize meal and salt on a tabletop. Make a well in the centre and gradually add the water. Use your hands to mix to a firm dough. Turn the dough onto a lightly floured surface and knead for a few minutes, or until smooth. Divide the dough into 6–8 portions. Roll out one at a time on a lightly floured surface until very thin. Keep partly covered with plastic to prevent them drying out.

Heat a heavy-based, non-stick pan and place one tortilla in the pan. When the edges begin to curl slightly, turn over.

Tortillas will soften while standing. Cut a greaseproof sheet into quarters and layer the tortillas with the sheets in between. They can be kept in a sealed container in the refrigerator and can also be frozen.

how to prepare a tortilla
Heat a little olive oil in a non-stick pan and gently fry the tortillas for about 1 minute per side. Remove from the pan and wrap in a dishcloth. Place them in the warmer drawer to keep warm and moist until you need them.

hints AND TIPS

- ✔ Salt aubergines before cooking to extract the bitter juices. Rinse before using.
- ✔ If you steam peeled aubergines before roasting or frying, it considerably reduces the amount of oil needed.
- ✔ For vegetables that grow beneath the ground, such as potatoes and carrots, start cooking in cold water.
- ✔ For vegetables that grow above the ground, such as beans, start cooking in boiling water.
- ✔ To improve the appearance of raisins, soak them in water for about 10 minutes to plump them up.
- ✔ Nutmeg and mustard improve the taste of béchamel sauce.
- ✔ It is not necessary to soak lentils prior to cooking. You should, however, rinse them first.
- ✔ To remove the bitter juices from ordinary cucumbers, seed and salt them for half an hour before using. Rinse well.
- ✔ Add sugar when cooking with tomatoes, and add mustard to cheese dishes to enhance the flavour.

- ✔ Add a raw potato to a soup or stew if it is too salty.
- ✔ Fresh parsley and coriander can be stored in a covered bowl of water in the refrigerator. Don't submerge the leaves and, if the coriander has roots, don't remove them.
- ✔ All ground spices, nuts and seeds can be stored in the freezer to retain flavour.
- ✔ Add cola to a chicken or meat marinade – it tenderizes the meat.
- ✔ When cooking with ham or gammon, add ginger ale to the cooking liquid.
- ✔ Duck eggs are great for baking.
- ✔ When baking, always use eggs at room temperature.
- ✔ Lemon grass can be replaced with lemon zest.
- ✔ To check if an egg is rotten, submerge it in water. If it floats, it is rotten.
- ✔ Oil a knife before cutting meringue.
- ✔ To check if an egg is hard-boiled, remove it from the water and place it on a tabletop. Spin it as you would a spinning top – if it flips up, it is hard-boiled.

- ✔ When making guacamole, place the avocado pip in the dip and cover. Refrigerate. Remove the pip just before serving.
- ✔ To store half an avocado, replace the pip, drizzle the avocado with lemon juice, cover and refrigerate.
- ✔ To remove a pip from an avocado, take a sharp knife and smack the pip with the blade. The pip will be impaled on the blade. Remove.
- ✔ Avocados will ripen more quickly if stored with apples and bananas.
- ✔ By pulping avocado and drizzling it with lemon juice, it can be successfully frozen in a freezer bag.
- ✔ Eat mangoes in the bath.
- ✔ To create a golden brown colour when baking, always use an egg wash.
- ✔ When baking, wipe down your tabletop with Jik water to kill the wild yeast in the air.
- ✔ Peanuts and bananas enhance your sex life.
- ✔ Toast nuts and seeds to improve flavour.
- ✔ When you have the urge to cook, invite a few friends.
- ✔ Do not skimp on quality.

- ✔ Marmite enhances most soups, gravies and stews.
- ✔ Never spend too much time in the kitchen – even at parties.
- ✔ When using stock cubes, remember to taste the dish first before adding more salt.
- ✔ Always sift your flour.
- ✔ To avoid dripping when ladling, scoop up a ladleful and dip it back into the soup or sauce. This will prevent dripping.
- ✔ Scatter fresh herbs onto the coals at a barbecue.
- ✔ Wear gloves when you're seeding and chopping chillies.
- ✔ Lemon grass, galangal, lime leaves and ginger can be frozen whole, then grated frozen into the food.
- ✔ Always use luke-warm water when baking bread.
- ✔ A draft is a killer for baking.
- ✔ Replace pine nuts with toasted almonds in a pesto sauce.
- ✔ To clean large quantities of garlic, place the cloves in boiling-hot water. The skin will peel off easily.
- ✔ When you burn your mouth with hot, spicy food, eat a piece of pawpaw to sooth your pallet.

essentials 37

"I love making soup because you can put anything into it."

soups

chicken stock
BASIC

makes as much as you need

1 leek, washed
celery leaves
1 carrot, washed
4 whole cloves
1 onion
a few bay leaves
1 whole chicken

First make a bouquet garni by tying the leek, celery leaves and carrot together with string. Press the cloves into the onion and place it in a pot together with the bay leaves. Add the chicken and the bouquet garni and top up with water. Bring to the boil, reduce heat and simmer until the chicken is cooked. Remove the chicken and strain the stock. Leave the chicken to cool, then remove the meat, discarding the skin, fatty bits and bones. The chicken can now be shredded for soups or can be used to make a great chicken mayonnaise sandwich. The stock can be frozen for later use.

"I usually use a vegetable stock cube or powder, but if the recipe requires cooked chicken I make my own stock from that. When using stock cubes or powder, always taste the soup before seasoning as the cubes tend to be very salty."

pumpkin, chicken
AND FIERY MOROCCAN PASTE SOUP WITH FRESH CORIANDER

serves 4–6

1 chicken, cooked in stock and shredded
4–6 cups (1–1.5 litres) Basic Chicken Stock (previous page)
1 large onion, thinly sliced
a small piece of ginger, peeled, crushed and chopped
3 Tbsp (45 ml) olive oil
2.5 kg pumpkin, cleaned and cut into cubes
a pinch of grated nutmeg
a pinch of ground cinnamon
4 tsp (20 ml) Fiery Moroccan Paste (page 19)
a large handful of fresh coriander
a pinch of white pepper
⅔ cup (160 ml) fresh cream
2 Tbsp (30 ml) castor sugar
salt (only if necessary)

Prepare the chicken and stock as described on the previous page.

In a deep pot, sauté the onion and ginger in the oil for a few minutes. Add the pumpkin, stock, nutmeg, cinnamon, Moroccan paste and half of the coriander. Bring to the boil, reduce heat and simmer until the pumpkin is cooked. Allow to cool slightly, then blend to a smooth consistency. Add the chicken, pepper, cream and castor sugar. Bring to the boil again, then taste and adjust the seasoning if necessary. Stir in the remaining coriander and serve.

(photograph on page 38)

thai chicken
AND VEGETABLE BROTH

serves 4–6

½ each red, green and yellow pepper,
   seeded and sliced
125 g baby marrows, thinly sliced
corn of 1 cob
125 g mangetout
1 sweet potato, peeled and thinly sliced
4 spring onions, thinly sliced
1 small butternut, peeled and cubed
2 Tbsp (30 ml) olive oil
2–4 Tbsp (30–60 ml) Green Thai Paste
   (page 15)
1 chicken, boiled and shredded
   (reserve 3 cups/750 ml stock)
1 Tbsp (15 ml) Basil Pesto (page 26)
2 x 400 ml cans coconut milk
salt and white pepper to taste
2 slices of lemon
a squeeze of lemon juice
2 lime leaves
a large handful of fresh coriander
1 x 230 g can bamboo shoots (optional)
a few drops of fish sauce

Sauté the vegetables in oil for a few minutes, then stir in the green Thai paste. Add the stock, pesto and coconut milk. Taste and adjust seasoning. Add the shredded chicken, slices of lemon, a good squeeze of lemon juice, the lime leaves, half the coriander, the bamboo shoots (if using) and fish sauce, and simmer gently (do not boil as the coconut milk will separate) until the sweet potato and butternut are cooked. If too mild, add a little more Thai paste, and if too fiery add coconut milk or stock to taste. Garnish with remaining coriander and serve.

soups

butternut,
CHILLI AND COCONUT SOUP

serves 4–6

1 onion, roughly chopped
2 cloves garlic, crushed
2 Tbsp (30 ml) olive oil
2 tsp (10 ml) ground chilli
2 tsp (10 ml) ground cumin
salt and white pepper
1 red apple, roughly chopped
2–3 large butternuts, peeled and cubed
5–6 cups (1.25–1.5 litres) stock
1 tsp (5 ml) Basil Pesto (page 26)
1 x 400 ml can coconut milk
a handful of fresh coriander

Sauté the onion and garlic in oil. Add the chilli, cumin and seasoning and stir for a few minutes. Add the apple, butternut and stock, bring to the boil, reduce heat and simmer until the butternut is cooked. Add the pesto and coconut milk, leave to cool slightly and blend to a smooth purée. Add coriander. Check seasoning. Bring to the boil again and adjust consistency if necessary.

thai chicken,
VEGETABLE AND BUTTERNUT SOUP

This combination of the Thai Chicken and Vegetable Broth (page 42) and the Butternut, Chilli and Coconut Soup takes more effort, but is really worth it as it tastes awesome. Give it a try.

You will need half and half for this combo. After you have added the chicken, basil and coriander to the Thai Chicken and Vegetable Broth, add the Butternut, Chilli and Coconut Soup. Bring to the boil and season to taste. You may need to add more coconut milk. Play around a bit until you achieve the desired consistency.

café food
AT HOME

sweet potato soup
WITH GARAM MASALA AND CORIANDER

serves 4–6

1 Tbsp (15 ml) olive oil

1 Tbsp (15 ml) butter

2 large onions, roughly chopped

2 cloves garlic, crushed and chopped

a large pinch of grated nutmeg

2 tsp (10 ml) garam masala

salt and freshly ground black pepper

1.2 kg sweet potatoes, peeled and cubed

a large handful of fresh coriander,
  chopped

5 cups (1.25 litres) vegetable or chicken
  stock (reserve ¾ cup/200 ml)

6 Tbsp (90 ml) fresh cream

4 tsp (20 ml) sour cream

Heat the oil and butter and sauté the onions and garlic for a few minutes. Add the nutmeg, garam masala, seasoning, sweet potato and half the coriander and cook for a while longer. Add the stock and simmer gently for about 45 minutes until the sweet potato is cooked. Leave to cool slightly, then purée with a hand-held blender and stir in the fresh cream. Gently reheat and add more stock for the desired thickness. Taste and adjust seasoning. Spoon the sour cream into the soup when serving, and top with a good sprinkling of fresh coriander.

bacon, gorgonzola and tomato soup with basil
and sun-dried tomato pesto

bacon, gorgonzola and tomato soup

WITH BASIL AND SUN-DRIED TOMATO PESTO

serves 4–6

2 Tbsp (30 ml) olive oil

1 large onion, chopped

2 cloves garlic, crushed and chopped

200 g bacon, chopped

1 carrot, peeled and roughly chopped

1 leek, roughly chopped

1 stalk table celery, roughly chopped

3 x 400 g cans whole, peeled tomatoes

freshly ground black pepper to taste

4 cups (1 litre) Basic Chicken Stock
  (page 40)

115 g gorgonzola cheese (this cheese
  is salty – so go slow on the salt)

3 Tbsp (45 ml) fresh cream

2 Tbsp (30 ml) Sun-dried Tomato Pesto
  (page 27)

2 Tbsp (30 ml) Basil Pesto (page 26)

sugar (only if the tomatoes are
  too acidic)

salt to taste

Add the oil to a deep pot and gently sauté the onion, garlic and bacon for a few minutes. Add the carrot, leek and celery and sweat off. Add the canned tomatoes, pepper and chicken stock. Bring to the boil, reduce heat and simmer until all the vegetables are cooked. Leave to cool slightly and purée with a hand-held blender until fairly smooth.

Crumble or grate the gorgonzola into the pot, and stir in the cream and pestos. Gently bring the soup to the boil. Taste and adjust the seasoning and consistency if necessary.

smoked chicken

serves 4

olive oil for frying
2 carrots, peeled and roughly chopped
2 leeks, roughly chopped
2 stalks table celery, roughly chopped
1 large onion, sliced
a pinch of chopped garlic
6–10 cups (1.5–2.5 litres) chicken stock
500 g split peas
4 large smoked chicken breasts,
  thinly sliced
a handful of chopped fresh parsley
1 tsp (5 ml) soy sauce
freshly ground black pepper
½ Tbsp (7.5 ml) Marmite

Heat the oil in a deep pot and sauté the carrots, leeks, celery, onion and garlic. Add the chicken stock and split peas. Bring to the boil, reduce heat and simmer until the peas are cooked. Leave to cool slightly, then blend the soup with a hand-held blender until smooth. Add the smoked chicken and bring back to the boil. Add the parsley, soy sauce, pepper and Marmite and stir. Taste and adjust seasoning. If the soup is not the correct consistency, add a little more stock and bring back to the boil.

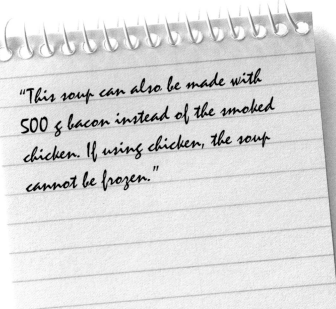

"This soup can also be made with 500 g bacon instead of the smoked chicken. If using chicken, the soup cannot be frozen."

smoked chicken and split pea soup

peanut butter,
VEGETABLE AND CHILLI SOUP

serves 4–6

olive oil for frying

1 onion, finely chopped

2 cloves garlic, crushed and chopped

1–2 tsp (5–10 ml) ground chilli

3 red peppers, seeded and neatly
  chopped into bite-sized pieces

4 carrots, peeled and neatly chopped
  into bite-sized pieces

3 stalks table celery (with leaves), sliced

4 potatoes, peeled and neatly chopped
  into bite-sized pieces

corn of 3 cobs

4–6 cups (1–1½ litres) vegetable or
  chicken stock

½ cup (125 ml) peanut butter

salt and freshly ground black pepper

a handful of fresh coriander

6 Tbsp (90 ml) fresh cream

Heat the oil and sauté the onion and garlic for a few minutes. Add the chilli and sweat off. Add the red peppers, carrots, celery, potatoes, corn, stock and peanut butter. Stir well and bring to the boil. Reduce heat and simmer for about 25 minutes until all the flavours have fused, but remember that the vegetables must remain crisp. Adjust the consistency with stock if necessary and add the seasoning and fresh coriander. Stir in the cream and serve.

thick chicken,
LENTIL AND VEGETABLE SOUP

serves 4–6

2 onions, sliced

2 cloves garlic, crushed and chopped

butter/oil combination for frying

2 carrots, peeled and roughly chopped

2 stalks table celery, roughly chopped

2 leeks, roughly chopped

1 x 400 g can whole, peeled tomatoes

**1 chicken, boiled and shredded as per
  Basic Chicken Stock recipe on page 40
  (reserve 6–8 cups/1.5–2 litres stock)**

**1–2 cups (250–500 ml) brown lentils,
  rinsed**

a handful of fresh parsley, chopped

salt and freshly ground black pepper

1 tsp (5 ml) Chilli Sauce (page 11)

a handful of fresh coriander

2 Tbsp (30 ml) Marmite

1 Tbsp (15 ml) soy sauce

a dash of fresh cream (optional)

a dash of freshly squeezed lemon juice

Sauté the onions and garlic in the oil/butter combination. Add the carrots, celery and leeks and sweat off, then add the tomatoes and chicken stock. Add the lentils, parsley, black pepper and chilli sauce and bring to the boil. Reduce heat and simmer until the lentils are cooked (about 30–45 minutes). Leave to cool slightly, then blend with a hand-held blender. Stir in the chicken. If the consistency is too thick, add more stock. Add the coriander, Marmite, soy sauce and cream (if using). Bring back to the boil and simmer for a further 5 minutes. Add a squeeze of lemon juice, taste and add salt if necessary.

salads

"At Gourmet Coffee House, the salads we serve are a meal on their own. They should be crunchy, fresh, tasty, texturally interesting and appealing to the eye – in other words, satisfying in every way."

christmas SALAD

serves 4–6

2 punnets oyster mushrooms

3 Tbsp (45 ml) olive oil

1 punnet cherry tomatoes, left whole

1 Tbsp (15 ml) Basil Pesto (page 26)

350 g assorted salad leaves (loads of
   butter lettuce, wild rocket, a handful
   of fresh coriander)

100 g chicory leaves

1 cup (250 ml) walnuts

50 g alfalfa sprouts

1 bunch spring onions, finely sliced

freshly ground black pepper

shavings of parmesan cheese

Cathrin's Lemon and Honey Dressing
   (page 30)

Sauté the oyster mushrooms in olive oil and set aside when cooked (try to retain their natural shape). Sauté the cherry tomatoes in the same pan with the basil pesto for 1–2 minutes. Place the lettuce on a flat platter and arrange the chicory leaves, walnuts, sprouts and spring onions on top. Grind over some black pepper and arrange the mushrooms and tomatoes on top. Sprinkle over shavings of parmesan and drizzle with dressing. Serve immediately.

potato
SALAD

serves 4

600–800 g new baby potatoes,
   cooked in salted water

DRESSING 1
1 cup (250 ml) plain yoghurt
a pinch of chopped fresh parsley
   and/or mint
3 Tbsp (45 ml) mayonnaise
a pinch of chopped garlic
salt and freshly ground black pepper
100 g feta cheese, cubed

DRESSING 2
a large handful of chopped
   fresh parsley
2 cloves garlic
1 cup (250 ml) freshly squeezed
   lemon juice
salt and freshly ground black
   pepper to taste
olive oil to drizzle
1 tsp (5 ml) Dijon mustard

First prepare the dressing of your choice by mixing all the ingredients together. Drain the cooked potatoes toss in the dressing.

"I always cook potatoes with their skins on and when ready I drain and rinse them in cold water. Peel them very quickly and toss them in the dressing. You can also leave the potatoes unpeeled if preferred, but scrub them well beforehand and boil until tender. If a sharp blade slides into the potato easily, then it is cooked."

smoked salmon
AND TARTARE SALAD

serves 4–6

350 g assorted lettuce, including a
  few spring dill
½ English cucumber, quartered and sliced
½ punnet cherry tomatoes, halved
500 g smoked salmon (reserve 100 g for
  the tartare)
a handful of alfalfa sprouts
freshly ground black pepper
½ onion, sliced into thin rings
1 lemon, quartered
Best-ever Vinaigrette (page 28)

TARTARE
½ onion, very finely chopped
1 small gherkin, finely chopped
4 capers, roughly chopped
a good squeeze of lemon juice
150 g smooth cottage cheese
reserved salmon, finely chopped
lots of freshly ground black pepper
a large pinch of chopped fresh parsley

First mix all the tartare ingredients together
and set aside.

Arrange the lettuce, cucumber and cherry
tomatoes on a platter. Place the smoked
salmon randomly over the salad. Spoon the
salmon tartare over the top and sprinkle with
alfalfa sprouts and black pepper. Top with the
onion rings and arrange the lemon wedges
on the side. Serve with the vinaigrette.

salads

teriyaki chicken
SALAD WITH VEGETABLES
JULIENNE

serves 4–6

350 g assorted lettuce
½ English cucumber, sliced
olive oil
4–6 chicken breasts (skinless),
  cut into strips
4–6 handfuls of vegetables suitable for
  stir-frying, such as carrots, baby
  marrows, mangetout, spring onions,
  mushrooms, baby corn, all thinly sliced
cherry tomatoes, left whole
freshly ground black pepper
a pinch of dried mixed herbs
a pinch of chopped fresh parsley
Teriyaki Sauce (page 18) to moisten
  while sautéing
a handful of alfalfa sprouts
Best-ever Vinaigrette (page 28)

Arrange the lettuce and cucumber on a platter. Pour the oil into a pan over high heat and add the chicken strips. Sear and seal, then add the vegetables, cherry tomatoes, pepper, mixed herbs and parsley. Drizzle over Teriyaki sauce and continue frying until the liquid has reduced completely. Brown the chicken and add more Teriyaki. When the chicken is cooked, sprinkle it over the salad and top with sprouts. Serve immediately with vinaigrette.

caféfood
AT HOME

crab sticks

WITH AVOCADO, PARMESAN CHEESE AND BASIL PESTO

serves 4–6

350 g assorted lettuce

4 crab sticks per person, sliced
   diagonally

1 carrot, peeled and thinly sliced

4 spring onions, sliced

250 g parmesan cheese shavings

250 g cherry tomatoes, halved

½ English cucumber, thinly sliced

2 Tbsp (30 ml) Basil Pesto (page 26)

2–3 ripe avocados, sliced

a handful of alfalfa sprouts

freshly ground black pepper

Cathrin's Yoghurt and Honey Dressing
   (page 30)

Arrange the garden greens on a platter
and top with the remaining ingredients,
ending with the avocado slices and sprouts
and a sprinkling of black pepper. Drizzle
with dressing and serve.

(photograph on page 52)

moroccan chicken
and roast vegetable salad

moroccan chicken
AND ROASTED VEGETABLE SALAD

serves 4–6

4–6 chicken breasts (skinless), thinly sliced
1 Tbsp (15 ml) Sun-dried Tomato Pesto (page 27)
2 Tbsp (30 ml) Fiery Moroccan Paste (page 19)
350 g assorted lettuce
½ English cucumber, quartered and sliced
125 g cherry tomatoes, left whole
1 bunch spring onions, finely sliced
6 Tbsp (90 ml) olive oil
4–6 cups Roasted Vegetables (page 31)
1 Tbsp (15 ml) Black Olive Pesto (page 27)
1 Tbsp (15 ml) Basil Pesto (page 26)
a handful of fresh coriander
a handful of alfalfa sprouts
Best-ever Vinaigrette (page 28)

Marinate the chicken breasts in the tomato pesto and Moroccan paste for 2 hours or longer. Arrange the lettuce, cucumber, cherry tomatoes and spring onions on a platter. Heat the oil and sauté and seal the chicken, then toss in the roasted vegetables and warm through. Sprinkle the chicken and vegetables over the salad and spoon the olive and basil pesto over the top. Scatter coriander and alfalfa sprouts on top. Drizzle with vinaigrette and serve.

gourmet's avocado,

PARMESAN, BLACK OLIVE PESTO AND GARLIC CROSTINI SALAD

serves 4–6

350 g assorted lettuce

75 g wild rocket

a small handful of fresh coriander

100 g parmesan cheese

1 clove garlic, crushed and chopped

2 small ciabattas, thinly sliced

6 Tbsp (90 ml) olive oil

1–2 Tbsp (15–30 ml) Black Olive Pesto
  (page 27)

4 spring onions, thinly sliced

a large pinch of chopped fresh parsley

50 g alfalfa sprouts

Best-ever Vinaigrette (page 28)

Arrange the lettuce, wild rocket and coriander on a platter. Using a peeler, peel strips of parmesan cheese and set aside. In a pan, gently fry the garlic and ciabattas in olive oil until crispy and golden brown. Add the crostini, pesto, spring onions and parsley to the salad and top with shavings of parmesan and sprouts. Drizzle with vinaigrette.

gourmet's avocado, parmesan, black olive pesto and garlic crostini salad

garden greens and
JULIENNE VEGETABLES TOSSED WITH CHUNKY COTTAGE CHEESE, AVOCADO AND WALNUTS

serves 4–6

**350 g assorted lettuce (I like to use lots
  of butter lettuce)**
3 spring onions, finely sliced
2 carrots, peeled and very thinly sliced
2 baby marrows, thinly sliced
125 g cherry tomatoes, left whole
½ English cucumber, quartered and sliced
250 g chunky cottage cheese
2 avocados
a handful of alfalfa sprouts
100 g walnuts
chopped fresh parsley
Best-ever Vinaigrette (page 28)

Place the lettuce on a platter and arrange
all the vegetables over the top. Spoon over
the cottage cheese. Slice the avocados
into quarters and arrange over the salad.
Sprinkle with alfalfa sprouts, walnuts and
parsley. Drizzle with vinaigrette and serve.

smoked chicken
WITH A MEDLEY OF FRESH FRUITS, NUTS AND CHEESE

serves 4–6

350 g assorted lettuce
150 g seedless black grapes
3 spring onions, finely sliced
150 g watermelon, seeded and cubed
100 g feta cheese, cubed
4–6 smoked chicken breasts,
thinly sliced
a handful of sunflower seeds,
lightly toasted
a handful of cashew nuts
125 g cherry tomatoes, halved
Cathrin's Yoghurt and Honey Dressing
(page 30)

Toss all the salad ingredients together and drizzle with dressing. Serve immediately.

caesar
SALAD

3 Tbsp (45 ml) olive oil

5 tsp (25 ml) butter

1 clove garlic, crushed

1 small ciabatta, finely sliced

1 cos lettuce

3 eggs, soft-boiled (2–4 minutes)

6 anchovy fillets, rinsed and finely
  chopped

a good squeeze of lemon juice

salt and freshly ground black pepper

100 g parmesan cheese shavings

DRESSING

2 cups (500 ml) Best-ever Vinaigrette
  (page 28)

½ cup (125 ml) fresh cream

5 Tbsp (75 ml) plain yoghurt

1 whole anchovy, chopped

1 tsp (5 ml) Worcestershire sauce

5 Tbsp (75 ml) mayonnaise

50 g parmesan or pecorino cheese, grated

1 clove garlic, crushed and chopped

First make the dressing by whisking all the dressing ingredients together in a bowl. Set aside.

Heat the olive oil and butter in a pan. Add the garlic and ciabatta slices and fry until golden brown and crispy. Set aside.

Finely grate one of the eggs. Tear the lettuce into bite-sized pieces and, in a mixing bowl, toss with the grated egg, anchovy fillets, lemon juice and seasoning. Drizzle with dressing and place on a serving platter. Cut the remaining eggs into quarters and scatter over the top with the crostini and parmesan shavings.

"Instead of using anchovy fillets, replace with slices of smoked fish, bacon bits or slices of smoked chicken breast. Be sure to use only cos lettuce."

chicory
SALAD

serves 4

It is important to make the dressing first. After washing the chicory, it must be tossed immediately in the dressing otherwise it will turn brown.

1 large chicory

DRESSING
6 Tbsp (90 ml) mayonnaise
1 Tbsp (15 ml) tomato sauce
a dash of Tabasco sauce
½ onion, finely chopped
1 Tbsp (15 ml) Black Olive Pesto
  (page 27)
1 Tbsp (15 ml) cognac or brandy
salt and freshly ground black pepper
  to taste

Prepare the dressing first by mixing all the ingredients together in a mixing bowl. Taste and adjust the seasoning if necessary as the black olive pesto may be too salty.

   Remove the heart from the chicory, wash well and drain. Toss with the salad dressing. Serve immediately.

WARMED roasted chillied butternut,
BASIL AND BLUE CHEESE SALAD

serves 4

250 g assorted lettuce

½ English cucumber, thinly sliced

125 g cherry tomatoes, sliced

a handful of fresh coriander

1 bunch spring onions, thinly sliced

4–6 cups Roasted Butternut with Chilli
   (page 32)

150 g blue cheese, grated

2 Tbsp (30 ml) Basil Pesto (page 26)

Cathrin's Yoghurt and Honey Dressing
   (page 30)

1 cup (250 ml) plain yoghurt

Arrange the lettuce, cucumber, cherry tomatoes, coriander and spring onions on a platter. Warm the chillied butternut in a pan and sprinkle it over the salad. Sprinkle the blue cheese over the top and spoon over basil pesto randomly. Drizzle with the dressing and serve the yoghurt on the side.

"Customers often ask for the
strangest taste combinations,
but when you try it,
all you can say is:
Wow, this is really delicious!"

wraps

breakfast WRAPS

serves 2–4

4 Flour Tortillas (page 34)
2–4 cups (500 ml–1 litre) Basic Tomato
Sauce (page 10)
2 red peppers, seeded and chopped
1 Tbsp (15 ml) Fiery Moroccan Paste
(page 19) or 1 Jalapeño chilli,
finely chopped
eggs
½ cup (125 ml) grated cheddar cheese
chopped fresh parsley

(photograph on page 70)

Prepare the tortillas as per the method
on page 34.

Heat the tomato sauce and peppers in
a pan. When it comes to the boil, reduce
heat and add the Moroccan paste or chilli.
Simmer for a few minutes. Poach the eggs
(as many as you like for breakfast) in the
sauce, covered, until cooked. Add the grated
cheese and spoon the mixture onto the
tortillas. Fold over and sprinkle with parsley.

fiery moroccan chicken

serves 2–4

4 Flour Tortillas (page 34)

1 Tbsp (15 ml) Fiery Moroccan Paste
(page 19)

1 Tbsp (15 ml) Sun-dried Tomato Pesto
(page 27)

2–4 chicken breast fillets (skinless),
cut into strips

4–6 Tbsp (60–90 ml) olive oil

2–4 cups Roasted Vegetables (page 31)

¼ cup (60 ml) Hummus (page 23)

¼ cup (60 ml) Tzatziki (page 20)

¼ cup (60 ml) Tomato and Chilli
Relish (page 22)

2 Tbsp (30 ml) sour cream

a handful of fresh coriander

½ avocado, sliced

Prepare the tortillas as per the method on page 34.

Combine the Moroccan paste and tomato pesto and roll the chicken strips in the mixture until well covered. Heat the oil in a heavy-based pan and sear and seal the chicken. Just before the chicken is cooked, add the roasted vegetables and warm through. Spread the tortillas with hummus, tzatziki and relish and divide the chicken between the wraps. Wrap up and top with sour cream, a little coriander and avocado.

lamb with spices,
SALSAS AND HUMMUS

serves 2–4

250 g leg of lamb, cut into strips
4 Flour Tortillas (page 34)
2–4 large handfuls of vegetables
   suitable for stir-frying, such as
   carrots, baby marrows,
   mangetout, spring onions,
   mushrooms, baby corn, all thinly
   sliced
6 Tbsp (90 ml) Hummus (page 23)
6 Tbsp (90 ml) Tomato and Chilli
   Relish (page 22)
6 Tbsp (90 ml) Tzatziki (page 20)
fresh parsley and coriander to
   garnish

MARINADE
1 Tbsp (15 ml) freshly squeezed
   lemon juice
3 Tbsp (45 ml) olive oil (reserve
   a little for cooking)
1 Tbsp (15 ml) Fiery Moroccan
   Paste (page 19)

¼ tsp (1 ml) ground saffron
1 Tbsp (15 ml) chopped fresh coriander
¼ onion, grated
1 clove garlic, crushed and chopped
a pinch of ground cinnamon
a pinch of ground cumin
¼ cup (60 ml) water

Combine all the marinade ingredients in a bowl, add the lamb and leave to marinate for 12 hours.

Prepare the tortillas as per the method on page 34.

Remove the lamb from the marinade. Heat the reserved oil in a heavy-based pan and sauté the lamb. Add the vegetables and cook until the meat is done. Spread some hummus, relish and tzatziki over the tortillas (reserve some to top the wrapped tortillas). Place the lamb and vegetables onto the tortillas and wrap up. Spoon the left-over hummus, relish and tzatziki over the wraps and sprinkle with parsley and coriander.

lamb with spices, salsas and hummus

chillied chicken
WRAPS WITH COLESLAW AND GARLIC YOGHURT

serves 2–4

2–4 large chicken breast fillets, pounded and cut into strips
¼ cup (60 ml) Chilli Sauce (page 11)
4 Flour Tortillas (page 34)
6 Tbsp (90 ml) olive oil
a small handful of chopped fresh parsley
a pinch of dried mixed herbs
salt and freshly ground black pepper
4–6 Tbsp (60–90 ml) Garlic Yoghurt
4–6 Tbsp (60–90 ml) Coleslaw
¼ cup (60 ml) Tomato and Chilli Relish (page 22)
chopped fresh coriander to garnish

GARLIC YOGHURT
1 clove garlic, crushed and chopped
1 cup (250 ml) plain yoghurt
salt and freshly ground black pepper
a pinch of chopped fresh parsley

COLESLAW
1 cup (250 ml) shredded white cabbage
1 carrot, peeled and grated
½ cup (125 ml) mayonnaise
a squeeze of lemon juice
a dash of Dijon mustard
a dash of honey
salt and freshly ground black pepper

To make the garlic yoghurt, mix all the ingredients together and refrigerate.

To make the coleslaw, mix all the ingredients together and refrigerate.

Rub the chicken with chilli sauce and set aside for 15 minutes. Prepare the tortillas as per the method on page 34. Add oil to a pan and sear the chicken over high heat. Add the parsley, mixed herbs and seasoning. Spread yoghurt, coleslaw and tomato relish over the tortillas. Add the cooked chicken and wrap up. Sprinkle with fresh coriander.

veggie wraps

serves 2–4

4 Flour Tortillas (page 34)

2 Tbsp (30 ml) olive oil

**2–4 large handfuls of vegetables suitable
for stir-frying, such as carrots, baby
marrows, mangetout, spring onions,
mushrooms, baby corn, all thinly sliced**

freshly ground black pepper

a pinch of chopped fresh parsley

a pinch of dried mixed herbs

Teriyaki Sauce (page 18) to deglaze

¼ cup (60 ml) Tzatziki (page 20)

**¼ cup (60 ml) Tomato and Chilli Relish
(page 22)**

¼ cup (60 ml) Guacamole (page 25)

100 g feta cheese, cubed

¼ cup (60 ml) sour cream

fresh coriander

Prepare the tortillas as per the method on page 34.

Heat the oil in a heavy-based pan or a wok. Stir-fry all the vegetables over high heat, sweat off and add the pepper, parsley and mixed herbs. Douse with Teriyaki sauce and cook until the vegetables are slightly tender. Spread tzatziki, tomato relish and guacamole over the tortillas and divide the vegetables between them. Add the feta and wrap up. Spoon sour cream over and top with coriander.

teriyaki
HERB-CRUSTED CHICKEN WRAPS

serves 2–4

4 Flour Tortillas (page 34)
2–4 large chicken breast fillets
dried mixed herbs
a pinch of chopped fresh parsley
freshly ground black pepper
olive oil
2–4 large handfuls of vegetables suitable
for stir-frying, such as carrots, baby
marrows, mangetout, spring onions,
mushrooms, baby corn, all thinly sliced
Teriyaki Sauce (page 18) to deglaze
¼ cup (60 ml) Tzatziki (page 20)
¼ cup (60 ml) Tomato and Chilli Relish
(page 22)
sour cream
fresh coriander

Prepare the tortillas as per the method on page 34.

Cut the chicken into strips and coat with mixed herbs, parsley and black pepper. Add oil to a pan or wok and sear and seal chicken over high heat. Add the vegetables and the Teriyaki sauce and cook for 2–3 minutes. Spread tzatziki and relish over the tortillas and add the chicken. Wrap up and top with sour cream and coriander.

whole brown mushroom AND
CREAMY SPINACH WRAPS

serves 2–4

4 Flour Tortillas (page 34)
4 large brown mushrooms
½ onion, chopped
olive oil and butter
1 clove garlic, crushed and chopped
a handful of chopped fresh parsley
salt and freshly ground black pepper
2–4 handfuls of cooked and shredded
  spinach
a pinch of dried oregano
a pinch of grated nutmeg
1 cup (250 ml) fresh cream
100 g mozzarella cheese, grated
50 g blue cheese, grated
1 tsp (5 ml) Basil Pesto (page 26)
1 tsp (5 ml) Sun-dried Tomato Pesto
  (page 27)
1 tsp (5 ml) Black Olive Pesto (page 27)
sour cream

Prepare the tortillas as per the method on page 34.

Cook the mushrooms and onion gently in olive oil and butter. Just before the mushrooms are cooked, add the garlic, parsley and seasoning. Add the spinach and toss together, then add the oregano, nutmeg and cream. Simmer to reduce the cream. Add the mozzarella and blue cheese and melt in to bind the ingredients together. Add the pestos, then taste and adjust seasoning if necessary. Divide the saucy mixture between the tortillas and wrap up. Spoon sour cream over and garnish with pestos and grated mozzarella. Serve with a side salad.

thai chicken
WRAPS

serves 2–4

4 **Flour Tortillas (page 34)**
2–4 **large chicken breast fillets, cut
into strips**
2–4 **Tbsp (30–60 ml) olive oil**
2–4 **large handfuls of vegetables suitable
for stir-frying, such as carrots, baby
marrows, mangetout, spring onions,
mushrooms, baby corn, all thinly sliced**
2–3 **cups (500–750 ml) Home-made Green
Thai Sauce (page 16)**
a **handful of fresh coriander**
50 g **cashew nuts**
30 g **sunflower seeds**

Prepare the tortillas as per the method on page 34.

Sauté the chicken strips in olive oil over high heat. Add the vegetables and sweat off. Add the Thai sauce and reduce heat. Simmer for about 5 minutes, or until the chicken is cooked. Divide the chicken and vegetable mix between the tortillas, reserving some sauce. Wrap up. Pour the remaining sauce over the wraps and garnish with coriander, cashew nuts and sunflower seeds.

thai veggie
WRAP

serves 2–4

4 Flour Tortillas (page 34)
2–4 Tbsp (30–60 ml) olive oil
2–4 large handfuls of vegetables suitable
   for stir-frying, such as carrots, baby
   marrows, mangetout, spring onions,
   mushrooms, baby corn, all thinly sliced
2–3 cups (500–750 ml) Home-made Green
   Thai Sauce (page 16)
50 g cashew nuts
30 g sunflower seeds
a handful of fresh coriander

Prepare the tortillas as per the method on page 34.

Heat the oil in a pan and sweat off the vegetables. Add the Thai sauce and reduce heat. Simmer for about 3 minutes until the vegetables are cooked but still crisp. Divide the vegetables between the tortillas, reserving some of the sauce. Wrap up. Pour the left-over sauce over the tortillas and garnish with cashew nuts, sunflower seeds and coriander.

chillied fillet

serves 2–4

**300 g fillet, cut into 4 medallions or
  into strips**
¼ cup (60 ml) Chilli Sauce (page 11)
4 Flour Tortillas (page 34)
4–6 Tbsp (60–90 ml) olive oil
salt and freshly ground black pepper
¼ cup (60 ml) Tzatziki (page 20)
**¼ cup (60 ml) Tomato and Chilli Relish
  (page 22)**
100 g cheddar cheese, grated
4–6 Tbsp (60–90 ml) Hummus (page 23)
a handful of fresh coriander

Marinate the fillet medallions or strips in the chilli sauce for about 30 minutes.

Prepare the tortillas as per the method on page 34.

Heat the oil in a heavy-based pan and sear and seal the meat on both sides. Add seasoning. Spread tzatziki and relish over the tortillas and sprinkle with grated cheese. Add the hummus and fillet and wrap up. Garnish with coriander.

curried baked bean
WRAPS

serves 2–4

*This original recipe is delicious with
Mexican fare (instead of refried beans),
but also makes a great meal on its own.*

4 Flour Tortillas (page 34)
1 onion, finely chopped
3 Tbsp (45 ml) olive oil
2 Tbsp (30 ml) medium curry powder
2 tsp (10 ml) crushed garlic
1–2 tsp (5–10 ml) crushed fresh chillies
a pinch of dried mixed herbs
2 x 420 g cans baked beans in
  tomato sauce
sugar and salt to taste
¼ cup (60 ml) Tzatziki (page 20)
¼ cup (60 ml) Tomato and Chilli Relish
  (page 22)
100 g cheddar cheese, grated
a handful of fresh coriander

Prepare the tortillas as per the method on
page 34.

In a pot with a lid, fry the onion in some
of the oil. When the onion is translucent,
add the curry powder and stir very rapidly
and thoroughly. You may need to add a little
more oil to prevent sticking. Add the garlic,
chilli and herbs, then the beans, adding a
little water to wash the tomato sauce out of
the can. Stir well, then reduce heat and
cover to allow the mixture to simmer. Stir
occasionally to prevent sticking and burning.
After about 10 minutes add salt and a little
sugar to taste. Simmer over very low heat
for another 15 minutes. (This filling becomes
more delicious with time.)

Spoon the bean mixture onto the tortillas.
Divide the tzatziki and relish between the
tortillas and sprinkle cheese over the top.
Wrap up. Garnish each tortilla with a little
relish, coriander and cheese.

jungle curry
WRAPS

serves 2–4

4 Flour Tortillas (page 34)

1 Tbsp (15 ml) vegetable oil

a handful of green beans, trimmed
  and halved

½ cup (125 ml) bamboo shoots

2–3 carrots, julienned

2–3 baby marrows, cut diagonally

100 g mangetout

125 g button mushrooms, halved

125 g baby corn, sliced

2–3 cups (500–750 ml) Home-made
  Red Thai Sauce (page 16)

1 tsp (5 ml) soy sauce

1 tsp (5 ml) Basil Pesto (page 26)

salt to taste

a handful of fresh coriander

Prepare the tortillas as per the method on page 34.

Heat the oil in a pan and sweat off the vegetables. Add the Thai sauce and reduce heat. Simmer and allow the sauce to reduce and the vegetables to cook. Add the soy sauce and pesto and adjust the seasoning. Divide the vegetables between the tortillas, reserving some sauce. Wrap up, pour the remaining sauce over the top and garnish with coriander.

filling IDEAS

These fillings can also be used for sandwiches, pita breads, ciabattas, focaccias, pagnottas or croissants.

- ✔ Camembert, roast vegetables and pesto
- ✔ Roast vegetables, feta and pesto
- ✔ Parmesan shavings, marinated artichokes and black olive pesto
- ✔ Asparagus, sautéed mushrooms and mozzarella
- ✔ Goat's cheese, roasted peppers, capers and onion
- ✔ Asparagus, rocket, Parma ham and shavings of parmesan cheese
- ✔ Moroccan-style marinated lamb strips sautéed with vegetables
- ✔ Brie cheese slices, Italian salami and black olive pesto
- ✔ Smoked chicken, pineapple and herbed cottage cheese
- ✔ Creamy avocado, mozzarella cheese, spring onion and bacon
- ✔ Roast beef, sun-dried tomatoes and mozzarella

- ✔ Roast beef, hummus and gherkins
- ✔ Biltong, herbed cottage cheese and avocado
- ✔ Hummus, sun-dried tomatoes and lettuce
- ✔ Hummus, toasted sunflower seeds and coarse sea salt
- ✔ Sun-dried tomatoes, mozzarella, smoked chicken, sautéed mushrooms and avocado
- ✔ Lettuce, tomato, sprouts, sautéed mushrooms, basil pesto, avocado or hummus
- ✔ Smoked ham, brie cheese and mustard
- ✔ Camembert, roast aubergine, sautéed mushrooms and pestos
- ✔ Smoked chicken, bacon bits and cheese
- ✔ Smoked salmon, herbed cottage cheese and salmon tartare
- ✔ Roast leg of lamb, hummus, tomato and chilli relish and tzatziki
- ✔ Mustard, chicken livers and sour cream
- ✔ Cajun chicken and tzatziki
- ✔ Cajun chicken, roast vegetables and pestos
- ✔ Creamed spinach, sautéed brown mushrooms, trio of pestos and mozzarella

wraps

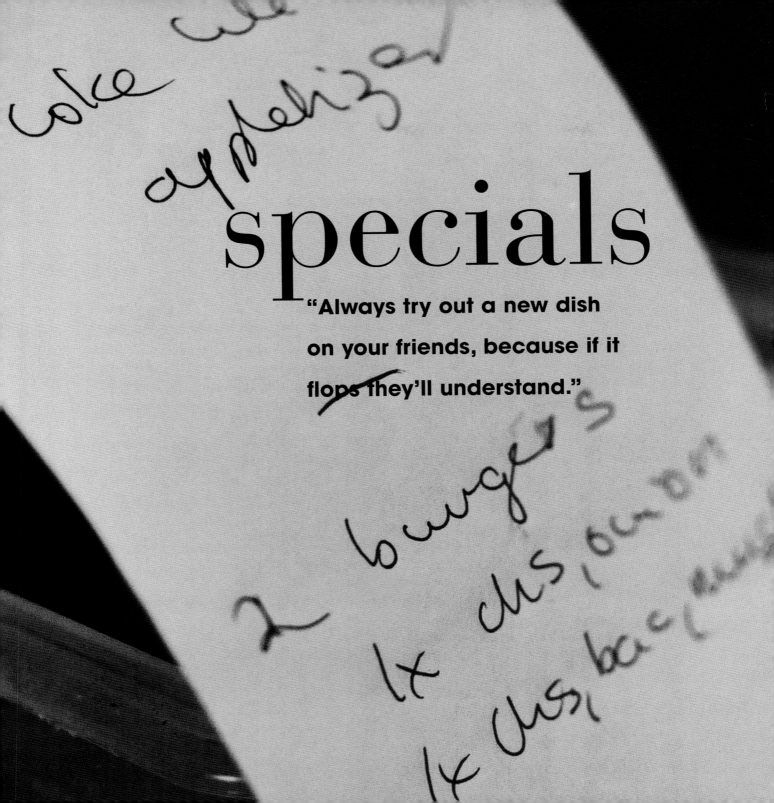

specials

"Always try out a new dish
on your friends, because if it
flops they'll understand."

cape salmon CAKES

makes 8

1.2 kg Cape salmon, skinned and filleted

5 Tbsp (75 ml) butter (reserve half
   for cooking)

1 tomato

½ onion

2 cloves garlic, crushed and chopped

5 whole black peppercorns

4 sprigs of fresh dill

4 sprigs of fresh parsley

1 lemon, halved

¼ cup (60 ml) white wine

6 Tbsp (90 ml) olive oil (reserve
   5 Tbsp/75 ml for cooking)

2 potatoes, peeled and boiled

a handful of chopped fresh parsley

6 drops of Tabasco sauce

4 eggs

salt and freshly ground black
   pepper to taste

6 Tbsp (90 ml) cake flour

1½ cups (375 ml) dried breadcrumbs

Preheat the oven to 180 °C (350 °F).

Place the salmon in a buttered ovenproof dish. Cut half the tomato and half the onion into thin slices and layer over the fish. Sprinkle garlic, peppercorns and sprigs of herbs on top. Squeeze over half a lemon and pour the wine over the fish. Drizzle with olive oil. Cover the dish with foil and bake for 15–20 minutes. Remove from the oven and set aside to cool.

When cool, flake the salmon, making sure you remove all the bones, and place in a mixing bowl. Grate the remaining onion and tomato and the boiled potatoes into it. Add the chopped parsley, Tabasco and 1 egg and mix well. Taste and adjust seasoning – you may need a little more lemon juice. Roll into eight balls and flatten slightly. Beat the remaining eggs. Coat the cakes with flour, dip into beaten egg and roll in breadcrumbs.

Heat remaining butter and oil in a pan and gently fry the cakes until golden brown.

SPICY MARINATED
roast leg of lamb

serves 6–8

3 kg leg of lamb, deboned and rolled
6–8 medium potatoes

MARINADE
2 large onions, very finely chopped
½ Tbsp (7.5 ml) crushed garlic
½ Tbsp (7.5 ml) ground cinnamon
5-cm piece of fresh ginger, peeled,
crushed and very finely chopped
½ tsp (2.5 ml) ground saffron
4–6 Tbsp (60–90 ml) Fiery
Moroccan Paste (page 19)
a large handful of chopped
fresh parsley
a large handful of chopped
fresh coriander
1 cup (250 ml) water
6 Tbsp (90 ml) olive oil
3 Tbsp (45 ml) freshly squeezed
lemon juice
salt and freshly ground black
pepper to taste

Place all the marinade ingredients in a mixing bowl and combine well. Put the lamb into an ovenproof dish and press the marinade mixture over the surface of the lamb. Allow some of the mixture to drop into the bottom of the dish. Cover and place the lamb in the refrigerator for 24 hours. Remove after this period and leave it to rest at room temperature for about 1 hour.

Preheat the oven to 180 °C (350 °F).

Peel and cut the potatoes and place them around the lamb, coating them with the marinade. Roast for 1½–2½ hours, basting and turning frequently until the meat is brown and crispy. To test if the lamb is done, stick a fork into the centre of the meat for a few seconds, then hold the fork against your lips. If it is warm, the lamb is medium-rare, if it is piping hot the meat will be medium done. Leave the lamb to stand for 10 minutes before carving.

beef burgers
WITH TOPPINGS

makes 6

3–5 Tbsp (45–75 ml) olive oil

6 burger buns

6 small side salads (tomato, lettuce,
   onion rings and cucumber)

BURGER MIX

1 kg regular beef mince

1 onion, grated

1 tomato, grated

2 slices white bread, crusts removed
   and softened in water

1 egg

½ Tbsp (7.5 ml) crushed garlic

1–2 tsp (5–10 ml) ground chilli powder

1 tsp (5 ml) ground cinnamon

1 tsp (5 ml) ground coriander

a very large handful of chopped
   fresh parsley

a good squeeze of lemon juice

1 tsp (5 ml) freshly ground black pepper

1 tsp (5 ml) salt

Work all the burger ingredients together and
mix very well with your hands. The longer you
mix, the nicer the burger. Divide into six balls
and flatten slightly.

   Heat the oil in a heavy-based frying pan and
seal the burgers on both sides over high heat.
Cook for about 20 minutes, turning frequently.
If you prefer them well-done, cook them for
an extra 10–15 minutes, turning frequently.

   Divide the salad between the buns, and
top with a patty and topping of your choice.
Close up the burger and serve.

IDEAS FOR BURGER TOPPINGS

– sautéed onion, cherry tomatoes and
   mushrooms
– cheese, sautéed mushrooms and bacon
– bacon, egg and cheese
– bacon, cheese and avocado
– Mushroom Sauce (page 12)
– all the above on one burger

beef burgers with toppings

gourmet's bangers
AND MASH

serves 4

2 Tbsp (30 ml) olive oil

8 thick pork sausages

1 clove garlic, crushed and chopped

1 large onion, sliced

250 g button mushrooms, quartered

2 Tbsp (30 ml) honey

1¼ cups (300 ml) red wine

a pinch of dried mixed herbs

1 cup (250 ml) Basic Tomato Sauce
   (page 10)

1 tsp (5 ml) Worcestershire sauce

3 cups (750 ml) water

1 tsp (5 ml) cornflour

1 Tbsp (15 ml) gravy powder

2 Tbsp (30 ml) fresh cream

salt and freshly ground black pepper

MASHED POTATOES

6–8 medium potatoes, peeled

6 Tbsp (90 ml) warm milk

2–3 Tbsp (30–45 ml) fresh cream

3 Tbsp (45 ml) butter

½ tsp (2.5 ml) prepared English mustard

a pinch of grated nutmeg

a pinch of chopped fresh parsley

salt and freshly ground black pepper

1 egg

Make the mashed potatoes first. Place the potatoes in a pot of cold water and bring to the boil. Cook for 30 minutes, or until easily pierced with a knife. Drain and place in a bowl. Mash with a potato masher, then add the remaining ingredients and continue mashing until light and fluffy. Keep warm.

Heat the oil in a heavy-based pot, brown the sausages, then set aside. Add the garlic, onion, mushrooms and honey to the same pot and braise for a few minutes. Deglaze with wine and return sausages to the pot with the herbs, tomato, Worcestershire sauce and water. Bring to the boil, reduce heat and simmer for 15–20 minutes. Stir cornflour, gravy powder and ¼ cup (60 ml) water into a paste and mix into the sauce to thicken. After a few minutes, stir in the cream, then check seasoning.

parmesan chicken strips
WITH CROSTINI

serves 4

2 small ciabattas, sliced
¾ cup (180 ml) olive oil
4–6 chicken breast fillets, cut into strips
1 Tbsp (15 ml) crushed garlic
a large handful of chopped fresh parsley
salt and lots of freshly ground
   black pepper
250 g parmesan or pecorino cheese,
   grated
1 cup (250 ml) Tomato and Chilli Relish
   (page 22)
2 Tbsp (30 ml) Basil Pesto (page 26)
balsamic vinegar to drizzle

Prepare the crostini by rubbing the ciabatta slices with olive oil and toasting them under the grill. Set aside.

Heat the remaining oil in a heavy-based pan and sear and seal the chicken over high heat. Add the garlic, parsley and seasoning. When the chicken is cooked, sprinkle over the grated cheese and mix well. Remove from heat and set aside.

Divide the crostinis between four plates and top with the tomato relish. Spoon the pesto over the relish and drizzle with balsamic vinegar and olive oil. Divide the chicken between the crostinis and grind more pepper on top. Serve immediately with a side salad.

easy roast chicken
AND VEGETABLES

serves 4–6

8–10 pieces of chicken
1 each red, green and yellow pepper,
seeded and thickly sliced
2 small sweet potatoes, peeled
and cubed
4 potatoes, peeled and cubed
50 g pitted black olives
1 small butternut, peeled and
thinly sliced
125 g cherry tomatoes, left whole
125 g brown mushrooms, quartered
1 onion, roughly chopped
8–10 cloves garlic, left whole
olive oil to drizzle
a few sprigs of fresh rosemary and thyme
½ cup (125 ml) water
a generous sprinkle of salt and freshly
ground black pepper

Preheat the oven to 180 °C (350 °F).
   Mix all the ingredients together in an ovenproof dish and roast for 1 hour, basting and turning the chicken often, until cooked and the skin has turned crispy and brown.

smoked chicken
PHYLLO WRAPS
ON MUSHROOM SAUCE

makes 8 (serves 4)

4 cups (1 litre) Mushroom Sauce (page 12)
**500 g smoked chicken breast, cut
  into cubes**
250 g chunky cottage cheese
150 g mozzarella cheese, cut into cubes
**2 tsp (10 ml) Sun-dried Tomato Pesto
  (page 27)**
100 g cooked spinach, finely chopped
200 g bacon, diced and cooked
2 tsp (10 ml) freshly ground black pepper
oil to brush phyllo
8 sheets phyllo pastry
grated parmesan or pecorino cheese
chopped fresh parsley

Prepare the mushroom sauce and set aside.
   Preheat the oven to 180 °C (350 °F).
   Using your hands, mix together the chicken, cottage cheese, mozzarella, pesto, spinach, bacon and pepper. Make eight equal-sized balls and set aside.

Brush oil directly onto a clean surface to the size of a phyllo sheet. Place one phyllo sheet on the surface and brush with oil. Place another sheet on top and oil again. Cut the sheets into quarters, place a ball onto each quarter and wrap up like a gift. Oil the surface again, place a phyllo sheet on top and brush with oil. Place another sheet on top and oil again. Cut the sheets into quarters, place the wrapped balls on each quarter and wrap again. Each ball should now consist of four layers of phyllo. Repeat the above method until you have eight phyllo wraps. Place the wraps on a baking sheet and bake for 25–30 minutes.
   While the pastries are in the oven, warm the mushroom sauce. When the phyllos are golden brown and crispy, remove from the oven. Ladle sauce onto each plate and place one or two phyllo wraps on top. Sprinkle with cheese and parsley and serve with a salad.

chillied butternut

WRAPPED IN PHYLLO PASTRY ON MUSHROOM SAUCE

makes 8 (serves 4)

4 cups (1 litre) Mushroom Sauce
  (page 12)
6 cups Roasted Butternut with Chilli
  (page 32)
100 g blue cheese, grated
2 Tbsp (30 ml) Basil Pesto (page 26)
oil to brush phyllo sheets
8 sheets phyllo pastry
a handful of grated parmesan or
  pecorino cheese
a large pinch of chopped fresh parsley

Prepare the mushroom sauce and set aside.
  Preheat the oven to 180 °C (350 °F).
  Combine the butternut, blue cheese and pesto in a mixing bowl. Roll into eight equal-sized balls and set aside.
  Brush oil directly onto a clean surface to the size of a phyllo sheet. Place one phyllo sheet on the oiled surface and brush with oil. Place another sheet on top and oil again. Cut the sheets into quarters, place a ball onto each quarter and wrap up like a gift. Oil the surface again, place a phyllo sheet on top and brush with oil. Place phyllo sheet on top and oil again. Cut the sheets into quarters, place the wrapped balls on each quarter and wrap again. Each ball should now consist of four layers of phyllo. Repeat the above method until you have eight phyllo wraps. Place on a baking sheet and bake for 25–30 minutes.
  While the wraps are in the oven, warm the mushroom sauce. When the pastries are golden brown and crispy, remove from the oven. Ladle the sauce onto the plates and place one or two wraps on top. Sprinkle with grated cheese and chopped parsley. Serve with a salad.

potato wedges
WITH SWEET CHILLI SAUCE

serves 4–6

8–10 medium potatoes
olive oil
1–2 tsp (5–10 ml) Cajun spice
sour cream

SWEET CHILLI SAUCE
¼ cup (60 ml) olive oil
1 bunch spring onions, shredded
2–4 green and 2–4 red fresh chillies,
  seeded and chopped
1 stalk lemon grass, minced
juice and zest of 1 lime or lemon
5-cm piece ginger, peeled and chopped
2 ripe tomatoes, chopped
1 cup (250 ml) brown sugar
2 Tbsp (30 ml) fish sauce
1 Tbsp (15 ml) soy sauce
4 cloves garlic, crushed and chopped
a handful of fresh coriander

Prepare the chilli sauce a few hours beforehand. Heat the oil and sauté the spring onions, garlic, chilli, lemon grass, zest and ginger very gently. Add the tomatoes and cook for a few minutes. Remove from heat.

In a heavy-based pan, add the sugar and a little water and melt the sugar over low heat. When melted, add the chilli-garlic mixture and the remaining sauce ingredients, and remove from heat. When slightly cooled, place in a blender and blend.

Preheat the oven to 180 °C (350 °F).

Scrub the potatoes and cut them into wedges. Place in a pot and cover with cold water. As soon as the water comes to the boil, drain the potatoes and place them in an ovenproof dish. Sprinkle with Cajun spice and drizzle with olive oil. Bake for 45 minutes, or until crispy and golden brown. Remove from the oven and serve with sour cream and the sweet chilli sauce.

BREDIE
butternut

serves 4

6 Tbsp (90 ml) olive oil
1.3 kg lamb knuckles
  or 750 g deboned lamb
2 onions, roughly sliced
2 leeks, sliced
5-cm piece of fresh ginger, peeled
  and chopped
3 cloves garlic, crushed and chopped
1 Tbsp (15 ml) ground chilli
2 tsp (10 ml) Fiery Moroccan Paste
  (page 19)
1 tsp (5 ml) ground cinnamon
a pinch of grated nutmeg
6 Tbsp (90 ml) white wine
6 Tbsp (90 ml) water
1 kg peeled and cubed butternut
a good squeeze of lemon juice
salt and white pepper to taste

Heat the oil in a large, heavy-based pot and sear and seal the knuckles until well browned. Add the onions, leeks, ginger, garlic, chilli, Moroccan paste, cinnamon and nutmeg and sweat off. Deglaze with the wine and water and simmer, covered, over low heat for 1½–2 hours, shaking the pot from time to time. Add the butternut and cover and cook for a further 30–40 minutes. Add the lemon juice and season to taste.

chillied butternut,
BLUE CHEESE AND BASIL LASAGNE

serves 4

3–4 cups (750 ml–1 litre) Béchamel Sauce
   (page 14)
250 g lasagne sheets
4–6 cups Roasted Butternut with Chilli
   (page 32)
2 Tbsp (30 ml) Basil Pesto (page 26)
100 g blue cheese, grated
1 cup (250 ml) grated parmesan or
   pecorino cheese

Preheat the oven to 180 °C (350 °F).

Pour a thin layer of béchamel sauce (about ¾ cup/180 ml) in the bottom of a rectangular ovenproof dish. Place one layer of lasagne sheets (about three) over the sauce. Spread half the butternut evenly over the lasagne and spoon pesto over randomly. Sprinkle a third of the blue cheese over. Repeat this process once more, ending with the béchamel sauce. Sprinkle over the parmesan or pecorino cheese and remaining blue cheese. Bake for 30–40 minutes. Remove from the oven and set aside for about 10 minutes before dividing into portions.

chicken and vegetable lasagne

chicken
AND VEGETABLE LASAGNE

serves 6

3 Tbsp (45 ml) olive oil

½ red and green pepper, seeded
and thinly sliced

1 onion, thinly sliced

125 g button mushrooms

1–2 cloves garlic, finely chopped

4 cups (1 litre) Basic Tomato Sauce
(page 10)

1 Tbsp (15 ml) Sun-dried Tomato Pesto
(page 27)

a pinch of dried mixed herbs

a large pinch of chopped fresh parsley

1 tsp (5 ml) soy sauce

1 tsp (5 ml) Worcestershire sauce

1 whole chicken, boiled and shredded

salt and freshly ground black
pepper to taste

3–4 cups (750 ml–1 litre) Béchamel Sauce
(page 14)

250 g lasagne sheets

1 cup (250 ml) grated parmesan or
pecorino cheese

Preheat the oven to 180 °C (350 °F).

Heat the oil in a heavy-based pan and sauté the peppers and onion for 2 minutes. Add the mushrooms and garlic and sweat off. Add the tomato sauce and pesto, mixed herbs, parsley, soy sauce and Worcestershire sauce. Simmer gently for 45 minutes to 1 hour. Add the chicken and bring to the boil. Taste and adjust seasoning. Remove from heat.

Pour a thin layer of béchamel sauce (about ¾ cup/180 ml) in the bottom of a rectangular ovenproof dish. Place one layer of lasagne sheets (about three) over the sauce. Spread half of the chicken mixture evenly over the lasagne and sprinkle with a little cheese. Repeat the method once more, ending with the béchamel sauce. Sprinkle with remaining cheese and bake for 30–40 minutes. Remove from oven and set aside for 5–10 minutes before dividing into portions.

lots of cheese

serves 6

1 x 500 g packet macaroni
2 Tbsp (30 ml) olive oil
½ onion, finely sliced
250 g button mushrooms, sliced
2 cloves garlic, chopped
a handful of cooked, shredded spinach
50 g blue cheese, grated
50 g mozzarella cheese, grated
100 g parmesan or pecorino cheese,
   grated
1 Tbsp (15 ml) Basil Pesto (page 26)
1 Tbsp (15 ml) Sun-dried Tomato Pesto
   (page 27)
1 Tbsp (15 ml) Black Olive Pesto
   (page 27)
4 cups (1 litre) Béchamel Sauce
   (page 14)
salt and freshly ground black
   pepper to taste
1–2 cups (250–500 ml) Basic Tomato
   Sauce (page 10)
a large handful of chopped fresh parsley

Preheat the oven to 180 °C (350 °F).

Prepare the pasta according to packet instructions, drain and place in a large mixing bowl.

Heat the oil in a heavy-based pan and sauté the onion, mushrooms and garlic for a few minutes. Add this mixture to the pasta, then add the shredded spinach. Add three-quarters of each of the cheeses to the pasta. Add the pestos to the béchamel sauce and pour over the pasta. Stir well to mix. Taste and adjust the seasoning. Place the pasta in an ovenproof dish, spoon the tomato sauce over the pasta and sprinkle with the remaining cheese and parsley. Bake for 20–25 minutes.

pasta with roasted vegetables, FETA AND PESTO

serves 2

250 g pasta of your choice, cooked
  al dente
1½–2 cups (375–500 ml) Basic Tomato
  Sauce (page 10)
1 tsp (5 ml) Basil Pesto (page 26)
1 tsp (5 ml) Sun-dried Tomato Pesto
  (page 27)
1 tsp (5 ml) Black Olive Pesto (page 27)
1 tsp (5 ml) Fiery Moroccan Paste
  (page 19)
2–3 cups Roasted Vegetables (page 31)
100 g feta cheese, cubed
salt and freshly ground black
  pepper to taste
1 avocado, sliced or cubed
50 g parmesan or pecorino cheese,
  grated

Cook the pasta, drain and set aside.

Warm the tomato sauce gently in a pan. Add the pestos and Moroccan paste and simmer for a few minutes. If at this stage the sauce becomes too thick, dilute with a little water. Add the cooked pasta and roasted vegetables and toss. Warm through. Add the feta and pepper. Taste and adjust the seasoning if necessary as the feta may be salty enough. Turn into a serving dish, top with avocado and sprinkle with parmesan or pecorino cheese.

penne
with mozzarella,
PESTO AND AVOCADO

serves 2

250 g penne, cooked *al dente*

1½–2 cups (375–500 ml) Basic Tomato
  Sauce (page 10)

2 tsp (10 ml) Basil Pesto (page 26)

2 tsp (10 ml) Sun-dried Tomato Pesto
  (page 27)

2 tsp (10 ml) Black Olive Pesto (page 27)

1–2 tsp (5–10 ml) Chilli Sauce (page 11)
  or Fiery Moroccan Paste (page 19)

100 g mozzarella cheese, cubed

a handful of chopped fresh parsley

salt and freshly ground black
  pepper to taste

1 avocado, cubed

50 g parmesan or pecorino cheese,
  grated

Cook the pasta, drain and set aside.

Gently warm the tomato sauce in a heavy-based pan. Add the pestos and chilli sauce or Moroccan paste and simmer for a few minutes. You may have to add a little water if the sauce reduces too quickly. Add the cooked pasta and mozzarella and toss. Warm gently and add the parsley and seasoning. Divide the pasta between two bowls and arrange the avocado on top. Sprinkle with the grated cheese.

penne with mozzarella, pesto
and avocado

cathrin's green thai PASTA

serves 2

250 g penne, cooked *al dente*
½ large red pepper, seeded and
   thinly sliced
2 Tbsp (30 ml) olive oil
4 large brown mushrooms, thickly sliced
½ cup (125 ml) fresh cream
4 baby marrows, sliced
2 spring onions, sliced
1 tsp (5 ml) Basil Pesto (page 26)
salt to taste
2 cups (500 ml) Home-made Green Thai
   Sauce (page 16)

Cook the pasta, drain and set aside (keep warm until ready to serve).

In a heavy-based pan sauté the red pepper in olive oil until soft. Add the mushrooms and sweat off. Reduce heat a little before pouring in the cream and simmer gently. Add the marrows, spring onions, pesto and salt. Stir in the Thai sauce, tasting to see if you need any more salt. The sauce should have a sweetish taste with a very fine aroma. Plate the cooked pasta and spoon over the sauce. If you like a hot sauce, add some Green Thai Paste (page 15).

crab penne

serves 2

250 g penne, cooked *al dente*
½ onion, thinly sliced
150 g button mushrooms, thinly sliced
1 tsp (5 ml) crushed garlic
6 Tbsp (90 ml) olive oil
2 Tbsp (30 ml) Chilli Sauce (page 11)
8 crab sticks, cut diagonally
1 Tbsp (15 ml) Basil Pesto (page 26)
lots of freshly ground black pepper
a squeeze of lemon juice
a large pinch of chopped fresh parsley
1 avocado, sliced
some lemon zest to garnish
100 g parmesan cheese, grated

Cook the pasta, drain and set aside.

Sauté the onion, mushrooms and garlic in the olive oil. Add the chilli sauce and crab. Sweat off for a few minutes, then add the cooked pasta, pesto, pepper, lemon juice and parsley. Toss well and warm through. Empty into a serving bowl and top with the avocado slices, lemon zest and parmesan cheese.

marinated fillet strips

serves 2

1 Tbsp (15 ml) **Fiery Moroccan Paste**
   (page 19)
1 tsp (5 ml) **Sun-dried Tomato Pesto**
   (page 27)
200 g beef fillet, cut into strips
250 g pasta of your choice, cooked
   al dente
2 Tbsp (30 ml) olive oil
a few slices each of assorted peppers
1½–2 cups (375–500 ml) **Basic Tomato**
   Sauce (page 10)
100 g parmesan cheese, grated
salt and freshly ground black
   pepper to taste

Combine the Moroccan paste and pesto. Add the fillet strips and marinate for 30 minutes. Cook the pasta, drain and set aside. Heat the oil in a heavy-based pan and sear and seal the fillet strips. Remove from the pan and set aside. In the same pan, sauté the peppers for a few minutes. Add the tomato sauce and gently bring to the boil. Add the cooked pasta and fillet strips and, when warmed through, turn into a serving dish and sprinkle with the cheese. Season and serve.

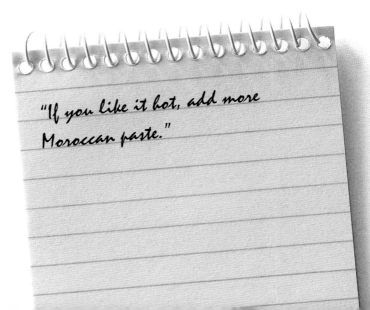

"If you like it hot, add more Moroccan paste."

"Eating something sweet
after a meal will get rid of
the urge to snack."

sweet
things

bread and butter
PUDDING WITH AMARETTO

serves 6–8

16 slices white bread
butter and apricot jam for spreading
90 g seedless raisins, soaked
  in Amaretto
½ cup (125 ml) Amaretto
8 large eggs
2½ cups (625 ml) milk
1 cup (250 ml) fresh cream
1 cup (250 ml) dark brown sugar
¾ tsp (4 ml) ground cinnamon
¼ tsp (1 ml) grated nutmeg

(photograph on page 116)

Make eight butter and jam sandwiches. Trim the crusts and cut into quarters. Arrange the quarters in a buttered rectangular ovenproof dish. Sprinkle with the raisins and drizzle with Amaretto. Beat the remaining ingredients together and pour over the bread, making sure the bread is soaked. Cover and refrigerate for 24 hours. Leave to stand at room temperature for 1 hour before baking at 160 °C (325 °F) for about 55 minutes until set and golden brown. When the pudding is removed from the oven, drizzle with more Amaretto if desired. Serve with fresh cream or ice cream.

HAYDEE'S
cheesecake

serves 6–8

1 x 200 g packet tennis biscuits
140 g butter, melted
2 x 397 g cans condensed milk
juice of 3–4 lemons
620 g smooth cottage cheese

Preheat the oven to 160 °C (325 °F).

Crush the tennis biscuits finely, pour melted butter over and mix well. Press the mixture onto the base and against the sides of a round ovenproof dish and refrigerate for about 15 minutes to set. Whisk the remaining ingredients together until well blended, then pour into the biscuit base.

Bake at 160 °C (325 °F) for 10 minutes and then at 120 °C (250 °F) for a further 10 minutes. Leave to cool, then refrigerate for 12–24 hours to set.

peanut brittle
BASKETS WITH CINNAMON

makes 4

½ cup (125 ml) castor sugar
a pinch of ground cinnamon
50 g unsalted crushed peanuts

"This is tricky and sticky so be very careful with the hot, melted sugar. You have to be very quick when making the baskets as the mixture cools down and becomes brittle and difficult to mould."

Place the castor sugar in a heavy-based pan over high heat. Stir continuously until the sugar has melted and changed to a golden brown colour. Stir in the cinnamon and crushed peanuts and remove from heat. Keep the stove plate on low as you may have to melt the mixture again.

Spoon half the mixture onto a clean surface, divide it in two and roll into balls. Flatten the ball with the palm of your hand and roll it out into a round. Shape over the underside of an individual muffin mould and pinch four corners into it. Leave to cool, remove from the mould and, *voila*, you have a basket.

Repeat the process with the other half of the mixture, so that you end up with four baskets. These baskets are beautifully decorative when filled with a dessert of your choice.

strawberries
AND PHYLLO

500 g fresh strawberries, quartered
¾ cup (180 ml) port
100 g butter, melted
4 sheets phyllo pastry
½ cup (125 ml) cream, whipped
3 cups (750 ml) ice cream
sprigs of fresh mint to decorate

Preheat the oven to 180 °C (350 °F).

Soak the strawberries in the port and set aside. Brush melted butter on a large clean surface and lay one phyllo sheet on top. Brush the sheet with butter and repeat until you have the depth of four sheets altogether. Cut the sheets into 12 squares, place each square on a baking sheet and bake for 10 minutes until golden brown and crispy. Remove and set aside to cool.

Using three squares per plate, take each square and fan it out so that each layer of phyllo consists of four separated sheets. Layer the strawberries, ice cream and cream between the phyllo sheets, ending with the third phyllo layer at the top. Decorate with a sprig of mint and serve.

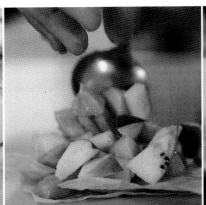

berry
SAUCE

makes 6–8 cups (1½–2 litres)

500 g frozen berries (reserve half)
250 g raspberry or strawberry jam
2–2½ cups (500–625 ml) white sugar
½ cup (125 ml) red wine
½ cup (125 ml) sherry
1 cup (250 ml) freshly squeezed
   lemon juice
1 cup (250 ml) water
2–4 Tbsp (30–60 ml) cornflour to thicken

Combine all the ingredients, except the cornflour and reserved berries, in a pot and bring to the boil, stirring from time to time. Simmer for 1 hour. Thicken with cornflour to the desired consistency and add the rest of the frozen berries. Return to the boil, then remove from heat and allow to cool.

   This sauce can be frozen and is great over ice cream, with cheesecake, over meringues or whatever your sweet tooth dictates.

carrot
CAKE

makes 2 loaves

2 cups (500 ml) sifted cake flour
1 tsp (5 ml) ground cinnamon
2 tsp (10 ml) baking powder
½ tsp (2.5 ml) ground ginger
½ tsp (2.5 ml) ground cloves
⅓ tsp (2 ml) bicarbonate of soda
1 tsp (5 ml) salt
4–5 eggs
1½ cups (375 ml) castor sugar
1 cup (250 ml) vegetable oil
3 cups (750 ml) grated carrots
½ cup (125 ml) chopped walnuts
½ cup (125 ml) sunflower seeds
¾ cup (180 ml) desiccated coconut

ICING
250 g icing sugar
2 Tbsp (30 ml) softened butter
250 g smooth cottage cheese
1 drop vanilla essence
a squeeze of lemon juice and some zest
  to taste

Preheat the oven to 180 °C (350 °F).

Sift the flour, cinnamon, baking powder, ginger, cloves, bicarbonate of soda and salt together, then set aside. In a mixer, add the eggs and castor sugar. Whisk on high for 3 minutes, then gradually whisk in the oil and blend well. Whisk for another 2 minutes or so. Fold in the dry ingredients with a wooden spoon and add the carrots, nuts, sunflower seeds and coconut. Divide the mixture between two loaf tins that have been sprayed with non-stick spray and bake for 35 minutes. Turn out on a wire rack to cool.

To make the icing, mix the icing sugar and butter, then add the remaining icing ingredients. Ice the cake and garnish with chopped nuts or grated carrot.

muffins

makes 6 large muffins

2 cups (500 ml) cake flour
1 Tbsp (15 ml) baking powder
½ tsp (2.5 ml) salt
½ cup (125 ml) dark brown sugar
1 cup (250 ml) milk
¼ cup (60 ml) oil
1 egg
1½ cups (375 ml) filling of your choice

FILLING IDEAS
- apple, toasted almonds and cinnamon with a sprinkle of nuts on top
- banana and nut
- apple, carrot, date, walnut and pecan
- date, nut and orange with zest
- chocolate (add cut-up chocolate and ½ Tbsp/7.5 ml cocoa powder to the dry ingredients and use hot coffee instead of milk)

Preheat the oven to 180 °C (350 °F).

Sift the flour, baking powder and salt into a fairly large bowl. Stir in the sugar. Pour the milk, oil, egg and filling into another container and mix well. Tip the wet mixture into the bowl with the dry ingredients. Fold everything together, taking care not to overmix. If the mixture appears too dry, add a little more milk – the mixture should be moist but not runny. Spray a muffin pan with non-stick spray and spoon the mixture into each mould until three-quarters full. Leave to stand for 15 minutes, then bake for 20–25 minutes. When you press the muffins, they should spring back. Cool and remove from moulds.

index

A

Avocado, Parmesan, Black Olive Pesto and Garlic Crostini Salad, Gourmet's 62

B

Bacon, Gorgonzola and Tomato Soup with Basil and Sun-dried Tomato Pesto 47
Baked Bean Wraps, Curried 86
Bangers and Mash, Gourmet's 96
Basil Pesto 26
Beef Burgers with Toppings 94
Berry Sauce 124
Béchamel Sauce 14
Bread and Butter Pudding with Amaretto 118
Breakfast Wraps 72
Bredie, Butternut 104
Burger Toppings, ideas for 94
Butternut
  Butternut Bredie 104
  Butternut, Chilli and Coconut Soup 44
  Chillied Butternut Wrapped in Phyllo Pastry on Mushroom Sauce 101
  Chillied Butternut, Blue Cheese and Basil Lasagne 105
  Warmed Roasted Chillied Butternut, Basil and Blue Cheese Salad 69

C

Caesar Salad 67
Carrot Cake 125
Cheese and Macaroni, Lots of 108
Cheesecake, Haydee's 119
Chicken
  Basic Chicken Stock 40
  Chicken and Vegetable Broth 42
  Chicken and Vegetable Lasagne 107
  Chillied Chicken Wraps with Coleslaw and Garlic Yoghurt 76

Easy Roast Chicken and Vegetables 98
Fiery Moroccan Chicken Wraps 73
Moroccan Chicken and Roasted Vegetable Salad 61
Parmesan Chicken Strips with Crostini 97
Smoked Chicken and Split-pea Soup 48
Smoked Chicken Phyllo Wraps on Mushroom Sauce 99
Teriyaki Chicken Salad with Vegetables Julienne 58
Teriyaki Herb-crusted Chicken Wraps 78
Thai Chicken and Vegetable Broth 42
Thai Chicken Wraps 80
Thai Chicken, Vegetable and Butternut Soup 44
Thick Chicken, Lentil and Vegetable Soup 51
Chicory Salad 68
Chilli Sauce 11
Christmas Salad 54
Coleslaw 76
Crab Penne, Gourmet's 113
Crab Sticks with Avocado, Parmesan Cheese and Basil Pesto 59
Cucumber Salsa *see* Tzatziki

D

Desserts *see* Sweet Things

F

Fillings, ideas for 88
Fish
  Cape Salmon Cakes 92
  Smoked Salmon and Tartare Salad 56

G

Garlic Yoghurt 76
Guacamole 25

H

Hints and Tips 36-37
Hummus 23

L

Lamb
  Lamb with Spices, Salsas and Hummus 74
  Spicy Roast Leg of Lamb 93
Lasagne
  Chicken and Vegetable Lasagne 107
  Chillied Butternut, Blue Cheese and Basil Lasagne 105

M

Macaroni, Lots of Cheese and 108
Moroccan Chicken and Roasted Vegetable Salad 61
Moroccan Paste, Fiery 19
Muffins 126
Mushroom Sauce 12

P

Parmesan Chicken Strips with Crostini 97
Pastas
  Cathrin's Green Thai Pasta 112
  Chicken and Vegetable Lasagne 107
  Chillied Butternut, Blue Cheese and Basil Lasagne 105
  Gourmet's Crab Penne 113
  Lots of Cheese and Macaroni 108
  Marinated Fillet Strips and Pepper Pasta 114
  Pasta with Roasted Vegetables, Feta and Pesto 109
  Penne with Mozzarella, Pesto and Avocado 110
Paste
  Fiery Moroccan Paste 19
  Green Thai Paste 15
  Red Thai Paste 15

Peanut Brittle Baskets with
    Cinnamon 120
Peanut Butter, Vegetable and
    Chilli Soup 50
Penne with Mozzarella, Pesto and
    Avocado 110
Pesto
    Basil Pesto 26
    Black Olive Pesto 27
    Sun-dried Tomato Pesto 27
Phyllo Wraps
    Chillied Butternut Wrapped in Phyllo
        Pastry on Mushroom Sauce 101
    Smoked Chicken Phyllo Wraps on
        Mushroom Sauce 99
Potato Salad 55
Potato Wedges with Sweet Chilli
    Sauce 102
Pumpkin, Chicken and Fiery
    Moroccan Paste Soup with
    Fresh Coriander 41
S
Salads
    Caesar Salad 67
    Chicory Salad 68
    Christmas Salad 54
    Coleslaw 76
    Crab Sticks with Avocado, Parmesan
        Cheese and Basil Pesto 59
    Garden Greens and Julienne
        Vegetables Tossed with Cottage
        Cheese, Avocado and Walnuts 64
    Gourmet's Avocado, Parmesan,
        Black Olive Pesto and Garlic
        Crostini Salad 62
    Moroccan Chicken and Roasted
        Vegetable Salad 61
    Potato Salad 55
    Smoked Salmon and Tartare
        Salad 56
    Teriyaki Chicken Salad with
        Vegetables Julienne 58
    Warmed Roasted Chillied Butternut,
        Basil and Blue Cheese Salad 69

Salad dressings
    Best-ever Vinaigrette 28
        with Sun-dried Tomato 28
    Cathrin's Lemon Dressing 30
    Cathrin's Yoghurt Dressing 30
Sauces
    Basic Tomato Sauce 10
    Béchamel Sauce 14
    Berry Sauce 124
    Chilli Sauce 11
    Home-made Thai Sauce 16
    Mushroom Sauce 12
    Sweet Chilli Sauce 102
    Teriyaki Sauce 18
Soups
    Bacon, Gorgonzola and Tomato
        Soup with Basil and Sun-dried
        Tomato Pesto 47
    Chicken and Vegetable Broth 42
    Peanut Butter, Vegetable and Chilli
        Soup 50
    Pumpkin, Chicken and Moroccan
        Paste Soup with Coriander 41
    Smoked Chicken and Split pea
        Soup 48
    Sweet Potato Soup with Garam
        Masala and Coriander 45
    Thai Chicken and Vegetable Broth 42
    Thai Chicken, Vegetable and
        Butternut Soup 44
    Thick Chicken, Lentil and Vegetable
        Soup 51
Stock, Basic Chicken 40
Strawberries and Phyllo 122
Sweet things
    Berry Sauce 124
    Bread and Butter Pudding with
        Amaretto 118
    Carrot Cake 125
    Haydee's Cheesecake 119
    Muffins 126
    Peanut Brittle Baskets with
        Cinnamon 120
    Strawberries and Phyllo 122

T
Teriyaki Chicken Salad 58
Teriyaki Herb-crusted Chicken Wraps 78
Teriyaki Sauce 18
Thai Chicken and Vegetable Broth 42
Thai Chicken Wraps 80
Thai Chicken, Vegetable and Butternut
    Soup 44
Thai Pasta, Cathrin's Green 112
Thai Paste, Green and Red 15
Thai Sauce, Home-made 16
Thai Veggie Wrap 82
Tomato and Chilli Relish 22
Tomato Sauce, Basic 10
Tzatziki 20
V
Vegetables
    Potato Wedges with Sweet Chilli
        Sauce 102
    Roasted Butternut with Chilli 32
    Roasted Vegetables with Red-Wine
        Vinegar 31
    Whole Brown Mushroom and
        Creamy Spinach Wraps 80
Vinaigrette, Best-ever 28
    with Sun-dried Tomato 28
W
Wraps
    Baked Bean Wraps, Curried 86
    Breakfast Wraps 72
    Chillied Fillet Wraps 85
    Chillied Chicken Wraps with
        Coleslaw and Garlic Yoghurt 76
    Fiery Moroccan Chicken Wraps 73
    Jungle Curry Wraps 87
    Lamb with Spices, Salsas and
        Hummus 74
    Teriyaki Herb-crusted Chicken
        Wraps 78
    Teriyaki Veggie Wraps 77
    Thai Chicken Wraps 80
    Thai Veggie Wrap 82
    Whole Brown Mushroom and
        Creamy Spinach Wraps 80